Rebirth of American Greatness

RESTORING FISCAL RESPONSIBILITY
AND MORAL INTEGRITY
TO OUR NATION

Peter Hughes

ISBN: 1477569723
ISBN-13: 9781477569726

Library of Congress Control Number: 2012909968

CreateSpace, N. Charleston, SC

I dedicate this book to my soul mate, best friend, and lovely wife, Alicia. We have been together since right after high school and I love her more today than ever.

Table of Content

Acknowledgments

As with my first book, *Death of the American Heart*, I believe my spiritual mentor, the Blessed Mother, has guided my hand. I asked her to guide me and to provide me with the wisdom and ability to communicate, with clarity, what is happening to our once-great nation.

Introduction

I need not tell you that we are in trouble as a nation. You know the signs, and on the news every night, you hear stories of a failing nation, a failing government, a failing educational system, and a failing society in general. Whether it is the high unemployment rate; government corruption; the high rate of home foreclosures; a failing economy; young women and children being abused, kidnapped, and murdered; or the general collapse of civility in our political discourse; these are the signs and forces at work that are contributing to our demise as a great nation.

Our once-great nation has lost its moral compass and vision. Our language has been degraded with obscenities that are used in music, films, books, and everyday discourse. Sexuality has replaced spirituality. Money and power have replaced compassion and caring. Love for self trumps love for others. In many social circles, it is okay to cheat and lie. The more public assistance we can get from the government, the better off we are, and it is not my money, so why not? The more we can cheat the customer or our fellow man, the better. The less work we can do and the more we can cheat our employers, the better off we personally will be, and why not?—they can afford it.

We have abandoned the great heritage that our ancestors created for us, as captured by the Declaration of Independence, the Constitution, the Bill of Rights, and the underlying values and principles that forged the platform to create such beautiful instruments of freedom and liberty. Instead of raising the bar of performance, accomplishments, expectations, and leadership, we have lowered the bar and inserted a socialist philosophy that government will take care of us and provide for us all that we need. We are taking from those that work hard and strive to do the best they can, and giving to those that only want a handout rather than a helping hand.

We have succeeded in stripping the symbols of God and religion from every public institution in America. God is no longer wanted or needed at the American public table of life. Good deeds have been replaced by greedy acts based on self-interest. Instead of embracing our elderly population, we sentence them to spend their last days on earth in drug-induced comfort-care cells rather than giving them the opportunity to spend just a little more time enjoying their families. We are spending our children's and grandchildren's national treasure on a wasteful government bureaucracy and wasteful government programs.

We have allowed our flagship manufacturing industry to be dismantled by greedy corporate executives and outsourced to China and India. This crime against our middle-class manufacturing employees was fueled by union officials who refused to embrace the necessary changes or concessions that would allow their organizations to maintain a competitive presence in the global marketplace. It was also fueled by corporate executives who were more concerned about their stock options and less concerned with investments in new capital and equipment that would save our jobs in America. We have choked off the growth of our small businesses by allowing the Washington bureaucrats to smother innovation and entrepreneurship with thousands of pages of forms, regulations, policies, and permitting requirements.

We have allowed our nation to become so politically correct that any of our traditions and holiday expressions that might be deemed offensive to someone will be stricken from the earth. Whether it is a prayer at a football game or graduation ceremony, or a painting of a traditional family unit on a school wall, it seems that it will be challenged as inappropriate. At one school, officials ordered the maintenance department to paint over a mural that a student had painted on a wall, with the school's permission, just because she portrayed a family consisting of a mother, father, and child. The school did not want to offend anyone who might be in an alternative family structure.

We have gone from having one of the best educational systems in the world to having one of the worst educational systems among the top twenty developed nations in the world. Our national debt is out of control, and nobody in Washington is doing anything about it because we cannot get along as a functional government.

We asked Congress to fix the problems, and Congress created the Super Committee to deal with our current economic issues. The two political parties could not work together and subsequently failed to put forth any solutions or recommendations to fix our nation's issues. Yes, there were hundreds of photo ops, and yes, there were many news conferences. Strong statements were made, but in the end, the Super Committee lacked the courage, fortitude, and leadership to recommend a single solution.

That is why I am writing this book. I am going to put forth the ideas, concepts, and recommendations that the Super Committee should have considered and debated. I am going to challenge Congress, the Super Committee, the Tea Party, and the Occupy Wall Street protesters to put aside their particular agendas and at least consider discussing solutions to our nation's crisis without bias, without preconceived paradigms, and without the mean-spiritedness that is currently part of our culture. I ask these groups to be open to listening to the ideas, concerns, and recommendations of the American people. I ask each of these groups to think, act, and work in the best interests of America. I ask them to put forth the effort, insight, and passion that will stop our economic, cultural, and political slide into a state of marginality. We are not Greece, Portugal, Spain, or a member of the European Community, so let's not drive our great nation into a state of mediocrity. Let's not give up our global leadership in science, technology, manufacturing, and medicine. Let's return America to a state of greatness.

There are two fundamental solutions that would address many of our problems as a country, and they are providing our children with a good and globally competitive education and providing our citizens with good jobs. Those two areas are the critical success factors for our sustained recovery as a nation. However, it will require a Congress and federal government to come together and put partisan politics behind them and focus on what is best for the future of our nation and the wonderful tapestry of citizens that represent its heart and soul.

For more than a decade now, while the two political parties and congressional leaders have been feuding, a darkness and emptiness has fallen upon our great nation. We have empty buildings in a state of decay that once stood tall and represented our industrial manufacturing leadership and innovation. They now languish in the quiet hours of their death. Our citizens have empty hearts that used to be caring, loving, and supporting of their neighbors and others in need. Now, they are filled with selfishness and a preoccupation with a "what's in it for me" attitude. We have empty minds. Minds that used to be filled with wisdom and worldly knowledge are now filled with selfish thoughts and mindless social clutter. We have empty souls. Souls that used to be filled with a sense of purpose and meaning are now aimlessly wandering in a sea of greed, hopelessness, and despair. The light of passion has been replaced with the darkness of self-absorption and evil.

We are becoming a pathetic society, degrading into a second-class country. We complain about everything that does not go our way. We do not accept responsibility for our actions and decisions. Our children have terrible role models shaping their behavior and moral character. Some TV, movie, and entertainment icons as well as super sports heroes behave in immoral ways and corrupt the young and innocent minds of our children with sex, violence, drugs, alcohol, and divorce, which they espouse through their behavior as the marks of "success." It seems as if it is okay, even very cool, to use profanity, to degrade women, and to exhort the virtues of violence in the rap music that our children listen to as their source of musical entertainment or as they study for school.

As the years pass, I continue to see our great nation slip deeper into being a society that honors greed over God. A society that is more concerned about blaming others than sitting down and solving problems. A society that permits evil to corrupt our children while condemning those who try to right the wrongs. A society that allows transgressions against the good people of our country while protecting the rights of the perverted. A society where it is more important to be politically correct than to honor traditional values. These are the conditions that stoked my heart with the passion to say we must stop this insanity, because if we don't, my children's children will suffer immensely.

I have written this book so that you, the readers, might find it in your hearts to get involved, to demand reform, to become agents for positive cultural change. I define you as American citizens who care enough for the welfare of your children, and your children's children, to take action. People who, because of your values and your passion, say enough is enough; we have gone too far and we need to reinvent our spirit as a great nation. The Super Committee was given a charter that it failed to execute. President Obama promised hope and change, and things have gotten much worse. Therefore, it is my hope that you, the readers of this book, will stand up against the corruption of our country's soul and with your voices, votes, and passion make a positive difference. We can and we must take back our country. The majority of Americans are desperately looking for both our political and our business leaders to create and drive the visions that will lead to our greatness as a caring, compassionate world leader. We cannot, and should not, leave our children in a morass of mediocrity. *We the People* will not let this nation travel down the path of time lacking a vision of greatness for America and all its wonderful citizens.

It is my hope that you will read this book and be energized to make a difference. Use the power of your social network to forward to your family members and friends those ideas that you believe have merit. The time has come. The melting pot is boiling with passion for change and transformation. We can make a difference. You can make a difference. Share this book with your family members and friends, and consider what you personally can do to make a positive difference.

Yes, you can, and yes, together we can make a profound difference to our destiny. There is no alternative road to our sustainable success as a nation. There is only one path to choose, and that path will lead us to the highway of success. It is this path that represents the beacon of light that will energize our souls and guide us on our transformational journey. Your destiny is to make a difference in this wonderful country of ours. And your journey starts right here, as you read on and become inspired with ideas that will shine the light of possibilities on the greatness of a new America.

Thank you, and please read on.

Chapter # 1

Recommendations for the Super
Committee and Congress

The leader of the House of Representatives and the leader of the
Senate, with the encouragement of President Obama, got together
and hand selected allegedly the best and brightest political minds
that both houses of Congress could offer. This dream team, which was
given the name "Super Committee," was chartered to develop a set of
recommendations to solve the economic problems facing our nation.
Committee members would work together to address and resolve the
serious issues and challenges that America faces today and the new
challenges it will face in the future. They would recommend sweeping
changes that would drastically reduce our spending, reduce our bulg-
ing deficits, and create a more prosperous future for all Americans.
Basically, the Super Committee was tasked to find 1.5 trillion dollars
that could be cut from the budget over a ten-year period.

So what happened? The Super Committee, aka the Political
Dream Team, met for months and did not come up with a single idea
that would address the critical problems facing our nation. Yes, indeed,
they met and yes, indeed, they debated, talked, discussed, explored
ideas, and held hearings—yet not one idea was implemented, or even
presented to you and me, the general public. The Democratic members
of the committee would meet privately and the Republican members
of the committee would meet privately, and then they would come
together with their parties' agendas and wind up in a stalemate. Our

best and brightest politicians from both sides of the hall were cursed with the sin of political ideology. Both the Republican and Democrat lawmakers were blinded by their political ideology as to what is in the best interests of America. They were deaf to the cries of the American people for changes that would stop the insane spending and wasteful behavior that goes on in Washington every day. Instead of embracing the types of reforms necessary to deal with the immense problems our country is facing, members from both sides of the political aisle clung to their own party's political ideology. Instead of thinking and acting in the best interests of the American people, they acted in the best interests of the union leaders, trial lawyers, Wall Street executives, corporate CEOs, and all the other special-interest groups who gorge themselves at the government trough of taxpayers' money.

The Super Committee failed the American people. The Super Committee failed all those brave Americans who gave the full measure of their lives defending our country. The Super Committee not only failed to develop a comprehensive set of recommendations and plans to get our country back into fiscal stability and prosperity; they failed to develop any plan at all. For months they played political games and postured for the news media coverage so they could slam the other party. Why have the media let them off the hook? Why did the media give the Super Committee a pass? Why are the majority of Americans not holding their feet to the fire of personal responsibility? The Super Committee failed because politicians in Washington do not care about you and me. They only care about themselves. They fight for airtime so they can talk about what they are doing and have done. They talk a very good game when the camera is on, but when the camera is turned off, that is when the hate speech starts toward the opposing members of the committee. They have deceived the American people. They have actually brainwashed many Americans with their political ideology. Those Americans blindly follow these politicians, excusing their lack of action and deeds as the fault of the other political party. Little do they know that their blind allegiance to the false words and broken promises is leading them down a road paved with hopelessness, despair, and a lower standard of living.

I became so frustrated with the Super Committee's inaction that I sent each one of them a copy of my first book, *Death of the American Heart*, which does contain some good recommendations for cutting costs and wasteful spending. But no one called, no one e-mailed, and no one said thank you. I, of course, did not expect to get a phone call or note of thanks. What I was hoping for was that someone would have said, during the discussions that were taking place in the committee meetings, that the American people expect us to come up with a plan, so let's put aside our political differences and work together to solve our problems. No, that did not happen because they did not care enough about our country to make the tough and difficult decisions required to right the American ship of state. They care more about party ideology and getting reelected than about what is best for America. It may not be a good analogy, and I do not want to offend anyone, but our country is like the Italian cruise ship that ran aground. Our great nation has hit the rocks, and it is listing deeply enough that it could sink if quick and decisive action is not taken. The captain and the crew have abandoned us and taken refuge in the lifeboats provided by the special-interest groups. They do not have the courage to help us, the American people, to guide us to safe shores, to right the ship of state and sail it once again into the sea of prosperity. The rats have left the ship and they are only thinking about themselves, their political party, and the special-interest groups who support their reelection campaigns. Their philosophy is, let the American people fend for themselves. It sounds like what Marie Antoinette said when confronted about the starving people of France: "Let them eat cake." Cake was the flour they put on the baking oven surface so that the baked goods did not stick to the oven floor.

So, I have decided to put forth what I think are the difficult decisions and recommendations the Super Committee should have made and presented to President Obama and Congress. To create a context before I present my recommendations, I need to frame who I am and what I do for a living. I currently have four jobs. My primary job is an organizational development consultant. As an OD consultant, I specialize in developing high-performing leaders and teams as well as improving the work processes they use to get their jobs done. I also teach part time at the University of New Hampshire's Whittemore School of Business and Economics and Cambridge College's Graduate School of Management. Finally, I am a freelance facilitator with The Browne Center, which is an organization that provides innovative experiential team-building and leadership-development programs to corporate teams and leaders. I consider myself to be an average American citizen. From a political standpoint, I am a novice and consider myself to be an independent and a member of the silent majority. I have never held a political office, but I have had many different leadership positions in business during my professional career. However, I do take an interest in what is happening to our country because I have eight grandchildren who will be impacted immensely by the decisions our government leaders make or do not make during the next few years. So, I thought that I would develop a set of recommendations and decisions that the Super Committee should have made or at least considered for a public debate.

I will first list the areas in which the Super Committee should have recommended substantial changes in order to get control over spending and the deficit. I will then elaborate on what I think needs to be done in each of the critical areas. Finally, I will merge the ideas contained in this book with the ideas in my first book, *Death of the American Heart*.

The list of areas the Super Committee should have considered for major changes are as follows:

1.   Social Security

2.   Balanced Budget

3.   Tax Structure

4.   Earmarks—One Bill, One Vote

5.   Health Care—Tort reform, Medicare and Medicaid fraud

6.   Downsizing Government

7.   Lobbyists

8.   Congressional Reform

9.   Deficit Elimination by 2022

10. Foreign Aid

11. Fanny Mae and Freddie Mac

12. Energy Policy—Oil Exploration, Coal, Solar, Wind, Geothermal

13. Manufacturing Policy

14. Right to Work Federal Mandate

15. Elimination of the Czars

16. Welfare Reform (SSI, food stamps, etc.)

17. Repatriation of Overseas Profits—Reinvest in American Operations

What I will do now is present the types of recommendations the Super Committee should have presented to President Obama and the Congress. I will start with Social Security as the first critical area:

1.   Social Security

a. Congress should immediately raise the retirement age for anyone under fifty to an eligibility age of seventy through 2020.

b. For anyone under fifty in 2021, Congress should raise the retirement age to seventy-two.

c. For anyone under fifty in 2035, Congress should raise the retirement age to seventy-four.

2.   Balanced Budget

a. Congress should immediately pass a law requiring the budget to be balanced every year after 2018. This would give our government and politicians five years to get organized and put the necessary discipline and structure in place to support the balanced-budget law.

3.   Tax Structure

a. A tiered tax system should be instituted, starting in 2015. Individuals who make less than $5,000 per year will not be required to pay federal income tax. Congress should adopt the following tax structure:

- $1.00–$5,000 = No Tax

- $5,001–$10,000 = 2%

- $10,000–$15,000 = 3%

- $15, 001–$20,000 = 4%

- $20,001– $40,000 = 10%

- $40,001–$60,000 = 13%

- $60,001–$100,000 = 16%

- $100,001–$250,000 = 17%

- $250,001–$500,000 = 18%

- $500,001–$1,000,000 = 19%

- $1,000,000–$5,000,000 = 20%

- $5,000,001–$10,000,000 = 25%

- $10,000,001+ = 30%

b. To support the proposed tiered tax structure, all tax deductions need to be eliminated, including the childcare tax credit, mortgage interest rate tax credit, energy improvements to your home tax credit, education credits, etc. *All* means just that: the elimination of *all* tax credits or incentives. The tax code should not be used to incentivize people to buy things or support political causes or projects such as "cash for clunkers." You should be able to complete your tax filing using a single one-page form from the IRS. It should be that simple. If the government wants to encourage citizens to support various programs and endeavors, they should use a grant system and leave the tax code alone.

c. The proposed tax structure is very simple. Again, you make X and you pay Y.

d. This new tax structure should free up a lot of staff employees at the Internal Revenue Service. Some of these employees can be downsized, while other IRS employees should be redeployed to focus on Medicare and Medicaid fraud as well as welfare and SSI fraud and waste.

e. The corporate tax rate should be reduced to 20%. This rate should also apply to profits generated from both domestic and overseas operations. However, if a corporation decides to repatriate those profits from its overseas operations and invest in new plants, equipment, and research and development (R&D) in the United States, the tax rate on those repatriated overseas profits should be 5%–10% since those profits will be used to create jobs in the United States. However, just as the personal income tax proposal listed above, this proposed corporate tax rate needs to be supported by a zero-exemptions policy. No loopholes or tax deductions of any kind. To stimulate research and development, we should use a grant-funding program such as we currently use to fund certain university research projects.

Since I am not an economist, the proposed tax structures for both individuals and corporations will need to be massaged, analyzed, and vetted to ensure fairness.

4.   Earmarks

a. There should be an immediate ban on all earmarks. Nothing should be added onto a bill. The philosophy in Congress should be "one bill, one vote." No attaching special appropriations to a bill. Every piece of legislation should stand on its own merit. We can create a budget for each committee to utilize for special appropriations or projects. However, each special appropriation or project will need to be discussed in committee and receive a majority vote. Every appropriation or project that is funded by a committee needs to be made public.

5.   Health Care

a.   The Affordable Care Act—or what a lot of people refer to as Obama Care—should be repealed immediately. A comprehensive health care plan is needed, but the current bill was flawed from the very beginning. The majority of American citizens did not want this particular health care reform program to become legislation; their demands ranged from killing the bill outright to redesigning the bill. However, their concerns and objections were ignored. The politicians we elected to go to Washington and represent us failed to acknowledge our voices. Nancy Pelosi, then-Speaker of the House of Representatives, stated that we needed to pass the health care bill so people could read the bill. This included both senators and congressional representatives, who needed to pass this legislation so they could then read what they had just passed. Does that make any sense to you? I don't think so. A bill was passed that the majority of American citizens did not want and that nobody read in its entirety. Now people are starting to realize how bad a piece of legislation the health care reform act really is, with all its hidden costs and taxes. Let us just focus on one little hidden tax that will negatively impact every American who sells his or her home after January 2013. If you sell your home after 2013, you will be required to pay a 3.8% tax on the sale. That represents an $11,400 tax on the sale of a $300,000 home. Is it any wonder that Nancy Pelosi, President Obama, and the Democratic Congress did not want anyone to read the bill before it passed? What about the $500 billion they are taking out of Medicare to help fund the bill? It is our senior citizens who will suffer the most, and yes, seniors, there will be government panels set up to regulate your treatment. Governor Sarah Palin referred to them as *death panels*. I won't go that far, but the panels will result in some seniors being denied certain procedures that would extend their lives because the procedures will be deemed not economically viable based on a cost-benefit ratio. Those seniors, if they themselves do not have the economic means to pay for the procedures, will be sent home with comfort-care provisions.

b. Here is what the Super Committee should have recommended.

- First, we need to repeal the health care reform act.

- Next, we must initiate major reforms to our tort system and put a cap on lawsuits. The current legal system is broken and is forcing many good doctors to leave their practices because of malpractice insurance costs and the number of lawsuits that certain lawyers are filing against them as practitioners.

- Once we have reformed our legal system, we need to aggressively address Medicare and Medicaid fraud. This type of fraud is costing the taxpayers hundreds of billions of dollars each year. It is blatant, out in the open, and we are not doing enough to stop it. I recommend that we unleash the IRS on the doctors, health care providers, hospitals, and clinics that are suspected of cheating the system. We can use technology to map and analyze claims and spot trends. As a result of the new tax structure put in place by Congress, many IRS agents will be available for redeployment to the front lines to fight fraud.

- One more major recommendation to address Medicare and Medicaid fraud is to establish mandatory jail sentences for people convicted of fraud. No plea deals; once a doctor, nurse, technician, office manager, or executive is convicted of fraud, he or she will go right to jail.

- Concurrent with the tort reform and fraud initiatives, we should have a joint committee redesign our health care system. This should entail taking the best parts of the current health care reform act and making the changes necessary to have a comprehensive plan that meets the needs of the average American citizen. No behind-closed-door negotiations, no input from lobbyists. No special exemptions for unions, corporations or other special-interest groups. Everyone will be required to participate in the plan, even Congress. Everything must be transparent and presented to the American people before any votes are taken.

- Finally, a new Super Committee should be created to focus only on health care reform. Too many Americans have been denied medical care by insurance companies because of previous conditions. Too many Americans have lost their insurance because they were laid off, and they find it very hard to get appropriate coverage while they are unemployed. Serious study should be given to a single-payer concept and insurance that people do not lose when they lose their jobs.

6.   Downsizing/Rightsizing Federal Government

a. A cabinet-level effectiveness review of every major program in each Secretary's area of responsibility should be instituted immediately.

b. Redundant operations, agencies, tasks, and positions should be eliminated. The goal is to reduce the size of the federal government by 30 %, in other words to the level it was when Bill Clinton first took office as president.

c. Technology should be incorporated and self-service kiosks implemented to reduce the amount of paperwork and the number of forms generated by government regulations.

d. Growth of the federal government should be capped at 25 % of the growth of our gross domestic product (GDP). For instance, if our GDP is 4 % the government growth could not exceed 1 % growth. If we have zero GDP growth, then the federal government could not expand.

7. Lobbyists

a. All lobbyists should be banned from Washington and required to conduct their business with senators and congressional representatives in the state offices.

b. Every lobbyist's visit to a senator's or representative's office should be made public, regarding who visited and the purpose of the visit. This information can be printed in the local newspaper or made available on the official's website. Transparency must be a requirement for all interactions with lobbyists.

c. Senior-level federal government employees must be banned from lobbying members of Congress for a period of five years after they have left office.

8.   Congressional Reform

a.   The congressional staff should be reduced by 30 percent.

b.   Senators and congressional representatives must be required to follow all the same laws that American citizens are required to follow. There must be no exemptions.

c.   Members of Congress should have the same health care and retirement plans as other federal employees.

d.   Revised term limits should be instituted, starting in 2016 with the presidential election. The president's term in office should be six years, a congressional representative's should be four years, and a senator's should be six years. This way nobody has to worry about getting reelected. Elections can be structured so that a third of the Senate changes every two years and half the House changes every two years.

e.   We should explore the possibility of doing away with the House of Representatives as we know it today. A panel should be commissioned to investigate the plausibility of reengineering our legislative branch of government to eliminate the House and expand the Senate. Is it possible for the legislative branch of our government to consist only of the Senate? What if we had five or six senators from each state instead of having House members as well as two senators? Could we dramatically reduce the bureaucracy, streamline the process of government, and reduce operating costs? I include this idea only as an interesting concept to think about and as an example of the type of breakthrough thinking the Super Committee should have engaged in regarding the quest to cut $1.5 trillion in ten years. Everything needs to be on the table for discussion. No sacred cows.

9.   Deficit Reduction

a. Congress needs to pass a law that requires the deficit to be eliminated by 2022. This would give the federal government sufficient time to manage its affairs and get its house in order. Whether by a constitutional amendment or a law, we need to transition to a debt-free nation by 2022. We should allow a deficit only if we are engaged in another war, we experience a major act of terrorism, or we need to deal with a horrific natural disaster from which we suffer a significant infrastructural loss that needs to be replaced ASAP.

b. Congress shall discipline the various agencies to spend only what they have budgeted to spend. Agencies and their employees should be incentivized to save money through process-improvement initiatives and rewarded when they come in under budget. The federal government will spend only what it takes in from its various revenue sources.

10. Foreign Aid

a. Congress should immediately pass a law which halts all foreign aid. We should continue to supply food, medicine, and clean water to friendly nations. We should not give aid to any country that does not like us, support us, or help us deal with global challenges such as Russia's and China's refusal to support the UN resolution to halt the killing of innocent civilians in Syria. As a result of these countries' refusal to support us, thousands more innocent men, women, and children were slaughtered. We should immediately stop all aid to Pakistan, which is working against us and, by its support of the Taliban, has indirectly contributed to the deaths of many of our servicemen and women in Afghanistan. We should also stop all foreign aid to China because it is not playing by the rules when it comes to global trade.

11. Fanny Mae & Freddie Mac

a. Congress should prevent the payment of legal fees to the former Fanny Mae and Freddie Mac executives who are charged with crimes. Congress should also abolish both Fanny and Freddie as quasi-government institutions. No taxpayer money should go to these organizations, and the government should go after the executives, current and former, to recapture some of the outlandish bonus money they were paid for managing these organizations into a state of deep decline.

12. Energy Policy

a. Congress should craft a comprehensive energy policy and send it to the president for his signature. We should open up all sites for drilling that have been identified as being viable oil-producing sites, including offshore sites and those in Alaska, Texas, and the Dakotas.

b. Our energy policy should include the use of coal wherever possible, with government grants being given for the development of clean-coal technologies.

c. A new generation of nuclear power plants should be built with a fast-track permitting process.

d. At the same time, the government needs to fund research for the development of alternative clean energy for our future requirements. However, we must exploit our current fossil-fuel resources as well as our nuclear resources until the clean-energy alternatives become a viable source. China is currently going around the world signing oil deals to make sure it has the necessary energy to continue to grow and prosper as a nation with the strongest economy in the world. We cannot let China out-negotiate us in the oil market. We also need to drill in our own backyard to reach a state of oil independence as a nation and not be held hostage by the Middle East and countries that teach their children to hate Americans.

e. We should immediately eliminate all subsidies to the oil companies. The top five oil companies had combined profits last year of approximately $137 billion. We should encourage drilling and exporting so they can continue to be successful, and at the same time we should redirect their tens of billions of dollars in subsidies each year to help pay down our national debt.

13. National Manufacturing Policy

a. Congress should create a robust national manufacturing policy, designed to protect our core manufacturing industries and entice companies to bring some of their outsourced operations back to the United States. The current global marketplace does not have a level playing field. Some countries, such as China, do not play by the rules. Other factors—such as our tax policy, environmental rules, enormous amounts of forms and paperwork, and the various regulations our manufacturers must comply with—put our companies at a competitive disadvantage. Congress needs to pull together a committee, consisting of the best academic and business minds, to help craft a manufacturing policy that will level the global playing field and eliminate the barriers that prevent our manufacturers from being competitive.

b. As I noted in my first book, *Death of the American Heart*, Congress needs to establish manufacturing enterprise zones in the poorest and most disadvantaged communities in the United States. Special tax incentives (reduced tax rates) should be given to any company that brings back a plant or operations that had been outsourced. The returning operations should be located within these newly created enterprise zones and would receive a substantial reduction in the tax rate on profits generated from these repatriated operations for some period of time (twenty years, for example). Some of you may recall the exodus of pharmaceutical companies that established operations in Puerto Rico and Ireland to take advantage of a twenty-year tax break. It is very possible for us to experience the same dynamic if we create the right type of incentives for companies to use these enterprise zones.

14. Right to Work

a. Congress should pass a law giving all American citizens the right to work anywhere and on any given government contract, private enterprise, or public institution. American workers, companies, and organizations of all types have been bullied by union leaders who are responsible for at least part of the drive to outsource American jobs to low-cost labor markets such as China, India, and Mexico. Unions' rigid work rules, their resistance to accept needed changes, and their refusal to respond to the dynamics of the new global market have put America at a competitive disadvantage. When Boeing wanted to relocate part of its manufacturing operation from Washington State to South Carolina, a right-to-work state, the company was told that it could not, and the government would take them to court to stop them from doing so. Who was driving this insanity? The unions, of course, because they wanted to keep union jobs in Washington. Apparently it is perfectly okay to let Boeing send its manufacturing operations overseas but it is not okay to allow them to send their operations to South Carolina. Given the current economic situation in this country, this move on the part of the unions and government bureaucrats defies logic.

15.   White House Czars

a.   Congress should recommend the elimination of all White House Czars and their respective staffs. These are the senior executives that President Obama has hired and placed in critical positions in the White House, bypassing the congressional approval process. At the same time, Congress should pass a law that requires anyone nominated by the president for a position in government to have a swift up or down vote. No playing politics and manipulating the nomination process to satisfy petty personal agendas. Let each nominee receive a swift yea or nay vote.

16.   Welfare Reform

a.   Congress should recommend comprehensive welfare reform. This reform should include a complete overhaul of the various areas that are subject to the largest amount of fraud and waste, such as food stamps, SSI, "Section 8" housing, and so on. How can over forty-two million Americans be collecting food stamps? Why are a significant number of disability claims based on mental disabilities? Whether it is Section 8 housing, SSI disability payments, general welfare payments, or food stamps, there are millions of people scamming the system—people who are quite capable of working but have chosen to sit at home and collect their government checks and benefits, while their greedy addiction to government benefits is being paid for by the majority of hard-working Americans. Not everyone is scamming the system. There are many people who need the help just to survive. It is not their fault that life has dealt them a bad hand. We are a compassionate people, when compassion is justified. One example of blatant abuse which represents a microcosm of the problem is an illegal alien in the Boston area who is living in government-subsidized housing, collecting a disability check, and enjoying other welfare-type benefits, while she is in this country illegally. How can this happen? Someone who is breaking the law is able to get government housing and collects a disability check. This situation underscores the need for comprehensive welfare reform.

I do not know how much money the above-mentioned recommendations would save if implemented, but I believe that they would exceed the $1.2 trillion that the Super Committee was supposed to recommend over a ten-year period.

Recently, I received an e-mail from a friend. You know the type: some you discard, some are inappropriate and you trash them immediately, and a few contain information that is thought provoking. One of these thought-provoking e-mails contained a video clip of talk-show host Chuck Woolery describing where he would cut the budget to save money and reduce the deficit. Mr. Woolery identified $1.5 trillion worth of savings in ten years. He went over the $1.2 trillion that the Super Committee was chartered to identify. Below is Mr. Woolery's list of items that can be either eliminated or reduced. The list is in no particular order and, like my list of recommendations, it will need to be vetted.

1. Eliminate the $90 million per year of free mail for Congress and have them use e-mail.

2. Eliminate the $146 million per year in first-class upgrades by federal employees.

3. Eliminate the $3.6 billion per year we give to run the United Nations.

4. Reduce the president's travel budget by $200 million per year.

5. Eliminate $30 billion per year in farm subsidies.

6. Eliminate $1 million per year that funds sanctuaries for Albino Squirrels.

7. Cut $30 billion per year from the Department of Energy by eliminating oil subsidies.

8. Eliminate $77 billion per year in funding for the Department of Education.

9. Eliminate $10.7 billion per year from the Environmental Protection Agency (EPA).

Total: 151,737,000,000 × 10 years = $1.5 trillion of savings.

How serious was Mr. Woolery's research? I would guess the depth of analysis was not to the level where you would actually implement his recommendations, but what about as a starter for discussion with the American people? Now, is it so difficult for the best and brightest senators and congressmen and women to come up with their own list of cost-reduction ideas? I believe it would not be that difficult for both groups and both political parties to identify their own lists of cost savings if they were willing to think and act in the best interests of America, not those of their party. Everyone in Washington will admit that waste is rampant in our government, but our senators and representatives refuse to do anything about reducing the wasteful spending and eliminating the redundancy throughout all of our governmental agencies, including the military. Instead of agreeing on ways to eliminate our national debt, our elected officials are fulfilling their governmental roles by increasing our taxes, increasing the fees we must pay for services, and increasing the amount of paperwork, forms, and bureaucracy that average Americans are required to deal with when we interface with the federal government. Our elected officials make simple transactions difficult, and difficult transactions impossible, but they cannot reach consensus on identifying areas to cut out of the budget that would reduce our federal debt and stabilize our country.

It is time that we take back our government from these money- and power-driven, corrupt government officials. Ladies and gentlemen, we are at a historical crossroads as a country. Depending upon which road we choose, it will mean the rekindling of American greatness or a rapid decline into the abyss of second-rate status behind India, China, Brazil, and several European countries.

Do we choose to be great again? Great innovators, great manufacturers, great educators, great scientists, great medical professionals, and a great and compassionate people. Or do we chose to saddle our children and grandchildren with a debt they will not be able to pay off in their lifetimes and a standard of living well below that which you and I have enjoyed in our lifetimes?

Chapter # 2

Outsourcing and the Decline
of Our Economy

Why is this topic so important to the future of middle-class Americans? Why should you even care about this concept? Many people do not realize what a significant negative impact outsourcing has had on our middle-class lifestyle, our tax structure, our national debt, and our ability to compete effectively in the global marketplace.

Outsourcing is the dagger that has pierced the heart of America. It has directly impacted our national debt, destroyed our tax base, fueled social spending on welfare-based programs, crippled our flagship manufacturing industries, marginalized the American worker, and eroded our global technology leadership.

Therefore, if outsourcing is so detrimental to the long-term prosperity of America, why have the best and brightest in Washington not addressed this horrific concern? There is a simple answer: greed. Money and power. These bedfellows are no strangers to the various players—just look who is sleeping together on the mattress of greed and you will find the same cast of characters: special-interest groups, Wall Street investors, corporate CEOs and their boards of directors, the blood-sucking politicians who want their pound of flesh, and of course, the almighty and powerful shareholders. I need to add context to the concept of outsourcing before I enter into the debate of how much profit is enough profit for a corporation. In addition, I will ask the question, do these corporations have a social responsibility to the communities in which their factories and offices are located, before they fire American workers and ship their jobs to cheap labor markets in places like India and China?

Organizations in the United States have engaged in some form of outsourcing since the eighteenth century. We became the dominant force in the textile-manufacturing industry. We had a very strong shoe-manufacturing industry supporting extensive leather-tanning operations. As shoe manufacturing was outsourced to other parts of the world, our steel industry started to gain world leadership. As textiles disappeared to third-world nations, the United States auto industry took off at an incredible pace. Thus, we lost shoe manufacturing and we lost textile manufacturing—no big deal; we were becoming world leaders in steel manufacturing and automobile production. Then our trading partner Japan started to dump its steel onto the US market at a lower cost than we could make it (even though Japan's steel-manufacturing industry was subsidized by its government). It was the start of the US steel industry's steep decline. This can of course be traced back to the industry's senior executives and union leadership. Because of the greedy way in which both parties conducted business, they in essence created a situation where we could not compete with the Japanese, and we lost our global leadership in the steel industry. Corporate executives refused to invest in the new technologies, new equipment, and new plants that were needed in order to be competitive. They were blinded by enormous salaries and incredible executive perks. The leadership of the union was corrupted by power, and it refused to effectively collaborate with management regarding changes in work rules and process improvements that were needed to stay competitive. Why should they give up the wage, benefit, and work-rule concessions they were able to negotiate from management, especially when they saw management still getting huge salaries and bonuses and enjoying all the executives' perks and trappings of office? Nucor Steel Manufacturing Company is a case study on how to run a successful steel mill. It is too bad that the big steel-producing companies did not have the same vision as Nucor.

The same exact scenario can be seen in the US auto industry. Its corporate executives and union leaders committed the same sinful, greedy acts, which led to a steep decline in market share for US automakers and gave the Japanese an incredible opportunity to be a serious player in the American automobile market. We lost our ability to compete. American automobiles cost more than their Japanese counterparts did, and the quality of the American cars was not as good as cars manufactured in Japan. This resulted in a significant loss of market share and fewer jobs in the auto industry.

However, even with the decline of both the steel industry and the auto industry, business executives did not worry because we were becoming expert at manufacturing consumer electronics and semiconductors. Once again, driven by stock-price pressures and cost-reductions initiatives, corporate executives saw an opportunity to outsource the manufacturing of consumer electronics to lower-cost labor markets, thereby reducing their operating expenses and increasing their profits. Still, this did not present much of a problem for the US economy or the middle class because the computer and software development industries were accelerating in their growth and providing significant and diverse job opportunities for our workforce. But guess what happened during this period in time—our corporate executives, pressured by Wall Street to keep their stock price high and pressured further by shareholders who wanted an even greater return on their investment, started to outsource their manufacturing operations, their design work, and their advanced software and information technology back-office operations to India, China, Taiwan, and other low-labor-cost countries. Starting in the '80s and accelerating during the '90s and through today, other companies began to outsource a wide range of operations that were deemed not to be core (critical to the strategic success of the business). Manufacturing companies felt enormous pressure from the big low-cost retailers to provide their products at a much lower cost if they wanted shelf space in the retailers' stores. This pressure drove manufacturers of commodities to outsource their manufacturing operations to cheap labor markets located overseas. If they had not done this, they would not have remained competitive and subsequently would not have survived in this global economy. The main motivation to outsource was finding cheap labor for manufacturing their products so they could stay price competitive. You will hear a different story from a lot of these companies as to their motivating forces. They will tell you that they could not find good engineers and scientists in the United States so they were forced to go to China and India. This argument simply is not true. We have an abundance of engineers in this country, many of whom have lost their jobs due to outsourcing. Often these displaced engineers must work below their intellectual capacity just to make a living. They cannot find work in their field of expertise because it has been sent overseas. The truth be told, our corporate executives have gone to China and India because they can pay workers from those countries significantly less than their American counterparts. In the end, it is all about exploiting cheap labor.

The big difference this time around is that there are no other up-and-coming industries to backfill the loss of computer, high-tech device manufacturing, information technology, and software-engineering jobs that have been outsourced to China and India. At the same time, these dynamic outsourcing forces are creating a negative vortex of energy in our economy; we are losing our bread-and-butter, core manufacturing industries. Go into any Home Depot, Lowes, Target, Walmart, or other warehouse retailer and look at the labels to see where things have been manufactured. You will be hard pressed to find much of anything that has a *Made in the USA* label on it. Whether it is a drill, a nail gun, a piece of pottery, a table, or a chair, the label is likely to bear the name of another country.

We have always been outsourcing, but we have always had an emerging industry to fill in and support our economic growth. Today we do not have that backstop industry, and at the same time, we are losing our core manufacturing industrial base. It has been said that the country that dominates the machine tool and die industry will be the dominant manufacturing force in the world. It used to be Germany, then it was the United States, and now dominance is slowly migrating to China. Why can we not build a smartphone in the United States? Apple sells hundreds of millions of smart devices from computers to iPads, yet we do not make them in this country. How much profit is enough? Has it boiled down to profit at any cost, even the loss of our middle class, the loss of our economy, the loss of our technological leadership in the world, and possibly the loss of our nation's status as a superpower? In the end, will it all have been worth it? Will the destruction of our way of life have been worth it?

We need to ask our political leaders and corporate executives a question: Is the extra profit, your extra bonus and stock options, or your ability to get reelected worth destroying the greatest nation to ever exist on the face of the planet?

Recently I had a debate with my son-in-law, whom I love deeply. He has a few investments, and we were discussing the particular issue of outsourcing our jobs and our critical industries to China and India. As a shareholder, he stated that he expects a maximum return on his investment. He does not see anything wrong at all with outsourcing our jobs to China and India. When I told him that I would be willing to pay a little more for a TV, cell phone, or computer that was made in the United States, he said he would not want to pay a little more and that that would diminish his financial return on his investment. He also stated that to make those devices in the United States would cost more than a few extra dollars when you purchased the device in the store. My counter argument was simple; I stated that I believe that companies like Apple, Dell, HP, and GE have a moral and social responsibility—to the United States and the communities where their plants and offices are located—to invest in automation and new technologies that will make those operations and processes more competitive. Rather than invest hundreds of billions of dollars overseas, companies could invest in new methods and training programs that would increase their competitiveness. We certainly will never be the low-cost producer, but we can be more competitive and it raises the question—how much profit is enough? How much of a return on your investment do you consider to be a fair return? Being more competitive sounds like being somewhat pregnant—you are either pregnant or you are not, and you are either competitive or you are not competitive. I personally think that given the opportunity, the American worker can be competitive and provide high-quality products and deliver exceptional customer service at a reasonable price point.

Having set the table of context, as biased as it is, I would like to profile the main forces pressuring organizations to outsource their manufacturing and service operations. Simply stated, the major forces are cost, employee benefit packages, environmental compliance factors, and finding cheap labor markets. The global marketplace dynamics are pressuring all companies to look at how they are doing things and find cheaper, lower-cost alternatives to running those operations. At the forefront of the lower-cost options is outsourcing operations to a lower-cost labor market. I wish I could say that the use of robots, new technologies, or process automation would be a viable option but I can't. Those alternatives represent a longer-term investment and a much longer return on investment.

The benefits of outsourcing are many and are extremely attractive to corporate management, the board of directors, and the shareholders.

- Operating expenses can be significantly reduced by taking advantage of cheaper labor overseas.

- Fixed assets can be eliminated, thereby adding additional cash for other investment opportunities. For instance, plants, equipment, and warehouses can be sold off, generating additional cash for operations.

- The organization can focus on its core business and strategies unencumbered by the daily issues and tasks generated by routine operations and the work environment. These daily tasks and responsibilities have been passed along to the outsourced company.

- Efficiencies can be gained in non-core processes such as purchasing, information technology, payroll, engineering, shipping, receiving, etc., because the non-core items have been moved to the outsourced partner.

- According to some experts, stress is reduced because mundane operations have been eliminated.

- There is more time for employees in the critical areas of the business to develop skills that they will need to master in order to support the core business strategies.

- Payroll costs are reduced, as are the expenses associated with the employees' benefit package. These particular cost reductions represent a significant savings to the bottom line.

- Management can spend more quality time on strategic issues and opportunities and less time on tactical issues and challenges.

- For a few employees this is a great opportunity to work with or provide support to the outsourced partner, which gives these managers and highly skilled employees some solid international experience.

- Raw material, work-in-process, and finished-goods inventory levels can be drastically reduced. Again, this will free up capital which can be used for other investment opportunities.

- Capital gains from freeing up assets from plants, equipment, and inventories, coupled with savings from reducing the workforce, create a very attractive investment propo-sition for Wall Street.

- On the new balance sheet, there are substantial increases in profitability.

- Corporate executives are excited because of the potential for some very large bonus checks based on performance improvements.

- Shareholders are happy because they experience a very good return on their investment.

- Wall Street is happy, and it is reflected in the stock price.

With all these positive benefits associated with outsourcing, why are so many Americans against outsourcing as an effective strategy? I will tell you why: because there are two sides to this particular coin. I just highlighted the benefit side of the outsourcing coin, but there is a downside to this concept that can negatively impact the organization and its managers, employees, customers, and shareholders.

- The biggest negative consequence of outsourcing is the loss of American jobs. Many hardworking, dedicated, and loyal employees have lost their jobs as a result of outsourcing.

- Many of those who have lost their jobs would never have even considered leaving their employer for another job with another company. They considered themselves to be employed forever until they retired. Now they find themselves out of work, and for some, it is the first time in their working lives that they are unemployed. The financial and psychological toll of unemployment is too great for some of these American workers to handle. Some have turned to alcohol and drugs to relieve the pain and embarrassment of not having a job. Some have committed suicide to escape from a life that has come crashing down on top of them. Others have experienced depression and spiraled down the staircase of hopelessness. Many find employment only to learn that they will be making a lot less money in their new job. However, with bills to pay and a family to feed they have no choice but to swallow their pride and accept the lower wage. Still others are working two and in some cases three part-time jobs just to make ends meet, but they have lost their medical benefits and cannot afford to purchase an individual family medical plan.

• Some of these laid-off employees have lost their home to foreclosure because they cannot afford to pay their mortgage.

• Others have had to tell their children that there will be no college because they need the money in the kid's college fund to live on while they seek employment.

• The self-esteem of these laid-off employees wanes and their self-worth plummets, but nobody in the corporate world seems to care.

- These laid-off employees will come to be known as the lost generation of American workers who were very productive and could have been even more productive but were denied the opportunity by greedy corporate leaders.

- Why don't we hear these stories from the media? I'll tell you why: they don't care. It is not politically correct to report the misery that millions of American workers are experiencing. When I talk about patriotism over profits, these are the Americans I am referring to, and when I say "how much profit is enough profit" I am referring to the mothers and fathers, sons and daughters who have suffered immensely as a result of job loss. What is preventing our corporate leaders from feeling the pain and suffering that their laid-off employees are experiencing? The only feeling these corporate leaders experience as a result of their strategic use of outsourcing is the feeling of elation that comes from the increase in compensation and bonuses they receive.

- If you go onto the Internet and research the concept of outsourcing—or offshoring, as it is referred to when operations are shipped overseas—you will find evidence that some individual companies are not seeing the types of cost savings they had hoped to see. As oil prices continue to rise, the cost of outsourcing production will increase, making it a less-attractive strategic option. Transportation costs as well as the cost of raw materials derived from oil will increase.

- Some companies have entered into agreements with outsourcing companies only to discover that it is not in their best interests to continue the relationship.

- There have been some legal issues with outsourcing companies over the rights to tooling necessary to manufacture the products. Other legal issues have centered on the rights to proprietary information and innovation.

- Not all is rosy on the outsourcing front. There have been issues with poor quality, poor service, and poor delivery of products, causing significant cost issues for the company and damage to the brand image of the company.

Outsourcing has presented significant long-term social, political, and technical challenges that must be addressed by both political parties and by corporate executives. I envision that these challenges will become so great that if we do not deal with them now, we will jeopardize the security and stability of this nation. Let me first tackle the long-term social implications. Our current unemployment rate is above 8 percent. You need to understand that the government is manipulating the numbers. We are not counting people who have given up looking for work, and we are factoring less-available jobs into the calculation—both of which tend to reduce the unemployment rate. If you calculate the unemployment rate based on how many Americans are out of work and are capable of working, the national unemployment rate is close to 15 percent. It is even higher in certain parts of the country and certainly much higher for some minority groups. With over forty-two million Americans on food stamps, with less than 50 percent of the American population paying any income tax, and with the significant additional cost of unemployment benefits and welfare programs, we are slowly becoming a welfare-dependent nation. This condition will spiral out of control, feeding the vicious cycle of poverty and crime, especially in our inner cities. Good jobs will solve a lot of our social issues, but social programs will not and cannot solve those same issues. A social program approach will perpetuate social unrest and keep families trapped in the cycle of poverty. We have a choice to make as a country: do we want to fill up our factories with workers or do we want to fill up our prisons with inmates? Our government and business leaders can choose to fill up our factories with employees by instituting the types of changes I am recommending.

With regard to the political implications of outsourcing, we are sending the wealth of our nation overseas to places like China and India. It will not be long before China becomes the dominant political force in the world in addition to having the most powerful military in the world. This spells disaster for the United States. We will not have the political clout in the future to influence geopolitical events. We will become subservient to China and lose our global leadership role. It will be a sad day for the world at large when this comes to pass— and it will come to pass unless our politicians and business leaders do something to stop it. That something is rebuilding our manufacturing capability to be the best in the world.

The technological implications are even worse than the other two (social & political). We are giving away our manufacturing, high-tech, and R&D secrets to many other countries in the world. We are teaching other countries our technologies, and they in turn will use those same technologies to compete against us in the global marketplace. Some of these countries don't even like us and what we stand for as a free nation. Whether it is manufacturing technology, supply-chain management, information technology, software development, new product development, R&D, medicine, or science, we have given it away. We have taught other countries how to use our technologies, and allowed those countries to steal or counterfeit our technologies. All of this downgrades our global technology leadership. We have partnered with Russia, China, India, and many European nations to have them design, develop, or build some of our most sophisticated electronics, aviation, computer, and software products. Many of these products have military applications. My goodness, the Russians don't even like us! We just witnessed both the Russians and the Chinese block a critical vote at the United Nations Security Council meeting to apply sanctions against Syria. As a consequence, thousands more Syrians were slaughtered. Why don't we just say to Russia, China, and Middle Eastern countries that we give up? Let's invite them in and have them dictate to us how we need to conform to a totalitarian approach.

Regaining our global leadership position in manufacturing, and turning the tide on the issues I mentioned above, will require leadership from our politicians, corporate executives, and union officials. If this triad sat down and developed a long-term policy not just to protect what is left of our core manufacturing base but also to reclaim our world dominance in manufacturing superior-quality products at reasonable cost and providing exceptional service, we will once again see a viable taxpaying middle class. Crime rates will be down, unemployment rates will be at record lows, tax revenues will be up, and most towns and cities will be prospering.

Listed below is what I think this new manufacturing policy will require from our politicians, business leaders, and union officials.

Our politicians need to

1. Create a tax policy that encourages investment in new plants, equipment, automation, and technology. This tax policy should apply to profits generated both within the United States and in other countries.

2. Create incentives for companies to bring outsourced operations back from overseas and relocate them in our most depressed communities.

3. Develop a policy that restricts governmental agencies like the EPA from placing new regulations on business without congressional approval.

4. Review all current regulations, policies, requirements, forms, and procedures, and eliminate those that are not adding value.

5. Create policies that make it easy to do business with the United States.

6. Place a 20% tax on all products imported from China.

Our business leaders need to

1. Look at investing in robotics and automation to upgrade their facilities.

2. Use outsourcing only as a last strategy. They need to explore lower-cost alternatives within the United States before they look to Asia or South America.

3. Refrain from paying bonuses or giving salary increases to executives who have generated profits on operations they have outsourced.

4. Force their purchasing departments to buy American-made products, sub-assemblies, and raw materials whenever available if the price is not too far out of line.

5. Implement formal cost-reduction programs in every one of their factories, offices, and operations.

6. Be willing to trade off some small measure of profit for the social good of the community before deciding to close a plant or operation.

7. Set a long-term strategic goal, if they are big warehouse-type retailers, to require 50 percent of the products they sell to be made in America.

8. Ensure that big electronic-device and computer-manufacturing companies manufacture no more than 50 percent of their products outside the United States. This 50 percent balance should also apply to IT, software engineering, web design, call centers, R&D, and other administrative functions.

Our union officials need to

1. Be flexible and willing to change work rules and proce-
    dures so the company can become more competitive
    and productive.

2. Be willing to give wage and benefit concessions rather
    than being rigid and forcing the company to go to China.

3. Participate with management as partners in the process
    of trying to keep plant operations open. This will require
    management to invite the union officials into their stra-
    tegic discussions and planning activities as trusted part-
    ners.

4. Encourage innovation by their members that will reduce
    operating costs and improve productivity.

5. Encourage their members to work hard and be flexible.

6. Embrace operational advances such as robotics and auto-
    mation.

To conclude this chapter, I would like to summarize the topic of
outsourcing by including some comments from my first book, *Death
of the American Heart.*

"What we have done to this nation over the last thirty years is
sinful. It is more than sinful; it represents the nail in the coffin that will
result in our demise as a great society and nation."

This quote highlights the fact that for the last thirty years we have sent millions of jobs overseas and started the great decline in our manufacturing economy and the dismantling of our middle class as we know it. We have eroded our tax base, weakened our national security, increased the stress levels of millions of American families, and diluted our global leadership.

"Our once-world-class manufacturing industry languishes in a state of continuing decline. Our once-proud manufacturing employees who worked for some of the most productive plants in the world sit quietly in deep despair, in a cold and insensitive unemployment office, waiting for an opportunity to return to a good job that provides a secure future."

This particular quote captures the past greatness of our manufacturing companies and their employees as being the best in the world, which was true at the time and still is true today when they are given the opportunity to perform.

"Let's bring back the pride of a label or sticker on a product that reads 'Made in America,' which means it was made with care, with quality, and by American workers."

This last quote focuses on the pride that our manufacturing employees demonstrated in the products they made and the services they provided. This pride equates to passion for their work and for their employers. There is nothing like a good job to lift someone's spirit. So, politicians please take note: if you want to solve the financial crisis we are in today, if you want to control deficit spending, if you want to reduce crime, if you want to increase our tax base, and if you want America to be a great nation once again, then reverse the outsourcing trend.

- Bring back our jobs and you will see a renaissance take place in this country.

- Bring back our jobs and you will see unemployment levels below 5 percent.

- Bring back our jobs and you will see the deficit slowly go away because of a robust tax base.

- Bring back our jobs and you will see crime rates drop substantially.

- Bring back our jobs and you will see a new collaborative effort in Congress.

- Bring back our jobs and you will see a resurgence in our housing market.

- Bring back our jobs and you will see Americans with renewed levels of pride, passion, and purpose.

- Bring back our jobs and you will see an explosion of innovation and technology breakthroughs.

- Bring back our jobs and you will witness America shift from being a welfare nation to being a producing nation.

- Bring back our jobs and you will see small communities, towns, and cities come to life again with a sense of purpose and pride.

- Bring back our jobs and you will experience a rebirth of our educational system as one of the best in the world.

We can accomplish all of these things with good jobs.

So, members of the Super Committee and other members of Congress, I ask you to create policies that will foster these types of changes. Members of the Tea Party and Occupy Wall Street groups, you need to passionately push for the reforms in laws, policies, and behaviors that will bring about these changes.

Good education and good jobs will lift the spirits of our nation. There is no downside, only a brighter future for America.

Chapter # 3

The American Cultural Shift and Personal Responsibility

What does the shift in the American culture have to do with the performance of Congress and the Super Committee? It in fact has a lot to do with the current level of dysfunctionality that exists in Congress and between the political parties. Understanding the cultural shift that has taken place in America over the last sixty years will help us to better understand our current economic decline and the level of dysfunction in our executive and legislative branches of government.

Since the Puritans set foot on American soil in Plymouth, Massachusetts, there has been the slow but steady creation of the American culture. To pay homage and give respect to Native American culture, I must note that it goes back thousands of years and encompasses many great tribes and nations. However, in the context of this book, I am going to refer to the period in history starting in 1620 on the cold and desolate shores of Massachusetts. I am going to focus on the culture building that has taken us to present-day America.

The Puritans brought with them a culture they considered to be free of impurities. To provide some clarity about what culture is and how it shapes a society, I offer the following descriptions. Culture consists of three dimensions or elements that tend to influence the thinking, behavior, and attitudes of a society: the things that you can see, the things that you can hear, and the things that you actually feel or experience. Culture sharpens social norms and influences the behavior of individuals, social groups, and demographically similar populations. There are national cultures, and within each nation there are many subcultures. Culture basically refers to a particular group of individuals or identifies how they behave—how they go about living their lives, demonstrating the social norms, values, and diverse nuisances that create the tapestry of their social group. While it may be an oversimplification, we can define a nation's culture as its personality.

Since 1620, we have been establishing and enhancing a core national culture. Every generation of Americans has contributed to the advancement of our national culture. Some of those contributions have been positive and some have not, in terms of their impact on our behavior. During our history as a nation, there have been many societal events that shifted and in a few cases transformed our national culture: all of the various wars we have engaged in as a country, as well as slavery, the Civil War, the Great Depression, the Industrial Revolution, the great immigration movement in the eighteen hundreds, the Transcontinental Railroad, the great western migration, the McCarthy era, the Cold War, President Kennedy's assassination, the civil rights movement, civil unrest of the '60s and '70s, rock and roll, the automobile, electricity, the computer, the 9/11 attack, and the Internet, to name a few. All of these events and their forces have imprinted on our nation's culture and created behavioral shifts within our society. What is alarming to me is the negative shift that has taken place since the '60s. There has been a steady degrading of the moral character of our nation as well as a growing level of disrespect for some of our country's core foundational values.

We no longer honor the sanctity of life. This is apparent not only in the killing of the unborn but in the constant killing of our citizens by their fellow Americans: gang killings, drive-by shootings, robberies that result in innocent men and women being slaughtered. It seems that every night Nancy Grace of the HLN cable news channel is covering a story about a young woman who has either been murdered or abducted. If the story is not about a young woman, then it is about a young child who has been kidnapped, sexually assaulted, and murdered. Just look at the number of men and women who are in prison for murder. It is the highest per capita rate in the developed world. When did we go so wrong as a nation? What events in our history have contributed to the lessening of the value of a human life? Why is it so easy for young people to resolve their differences with others by killing them? There has been a recent rash of men killing their wives and parents killing their children. Why? Why not divorce your wife instead of killing her? Why not kill yourself instead of your kids? It just does not make any sense. We must explore the core concepts of morality and decency as they relate to the shift in the American culture. Studying this culture shift will help us to understand our economic decline and our dysfunctional federal government. I believe they are interrelated, acting as negative feedback loops in a much larger system.

When I was growing up you could not say the word *damn* on TV or radio or in the movies, let alone the plethora of four-letter words and obscene language that is standard for movies, TV, DVDs, and radio today. There was no nudity on the big screen. There was no inappropriate language spoken. There were no video games or rap songs degrading women or spewing out the most hateful and obscene language. There were no TV shows like *Jersey Shore,* in which it is okay to get drunk and behave in ways that do not model the standards of morality and decency that we would like our children to embrace. A good number of TV shows today disrespect the family as a moral unit. They cast the father as a stupid moron and the mother as an oversexed, unloved woman starving for love and affection. Let's review just one of the basic foundations of culture: language. Our language has been corrupted by the inclusion of obscenities designed to punctuate or underscore a particular point. However, I find that inclusion of foul and vulgar obscenities in our daily communications is just an excuse to allow people to be disrespectful to others. It is not needed nor is it desired. It reinforces some deeper issues that center around our cultural behavioral norms.

As a member of any culture, you go through a period of cultural assimilation during which your behavior is influenced by your parents, siblings, family members, friends, social environment, schools, religious institutions, and the various forms of media. So why are these people and institutions not having a more positive affect on some members of our society? The answer is simple, the solution is complex. Over the past fifty years, there has been a constant attempt by liberals and the liberal media to purge anything that is associated with religion, God, or Christianity. Under the umbrella of being politically correct and not wanting to offend any particular group, no matter how small the group, the liberals of America started their crusade. From school prayer to the Christmas tree, anything that could be construed to have an affiliation with religion has been under attack, with attempts to remove it from our social institutions. Whether it is a cross in the desert of the Southwest or a cross hung over a battlefield hospital tent in Afghanistan, certain people wants those symbols removed, and they are getting their way. Recently, a school district in Massachusetts wanted the word *God* removed from the phrase *God Bless America*. In this case, they did not get their way, but they are still waging war against religion.

During this same period, when the extreme left has been campaigning for the disintermediation of our religious symbols, words, and prayers, we have embraced obscene language, violence, nudity in movies, and sexually explicit material throughout the various media. It is not difficult to correlate the purging of our religious heritage from our society with the moral decay we are experiencing. In addition, we have transitioned from the Greatest Generation to the Me Generation. In days past, the philosophy was to help your neighbor and fellow citizen. It was to share and do good deeds for those in need. Today it is all about *me*. What can I do to advance my lot in life? How can I get the most out of the government or my employer by putting in the least amount of effort? It is about scamming the system, cheating, being dishonest, and benefitting at the expense of others. In today's greed-driven world, a lot of Americans are not thinking about others, they are only thinking about themselves—and this includes our politicians. Today, over forty-two million Americans are on food stamps and a significant number of Americans receive some form of government-housing assistance or collect disability checks when they are capable of working—examples of *all about me* cultural behavior.

Once again, I need to point out the correlation between the decline of anything religious or Christian and the increase in social-welfare support and the millions of Americans who are cheating and scamming the system for personal gain. Some of these cheaters and scammers are professional people with law or medical degrees. Many have made it their full-time profession to see how much government assistance they can receive, and for how long they can get away with their illegal activities, especially in the case of Medicare and Medicaid fraud. Our grandparents and parents never looked for a handout. They found a way to support their families. It might have meant working two or three jobs, but they made the sacrifice. There was a great sense of pride and purpose in their lives. It was never about them, it was always about their families and communities. Today, thanks to the liberalization of America, it is too easy to get welfare assistance and too easy to become trapped by and fully reliant on government assistance.

Let me be perfectly clear: I am not castigating the poor among us. Nor am I criticizing the deserving and needy families and people who need support. I am referring to the people who are quite capable of working but who choose to play the system and have the government support them. We all know some of them—some might be right next door. Some work under the table and continue to collect government assistance. Others claim disability but are not disabled. The only thing that is disabled about some of these people is their conscience and their sense of right and wrong. We have created the illusion that there is nothing wrong with accepting government assistance even if you don't need it. You win the lottery but still collect your food stamps. How outrageous and un-American.

These societal trends and cultural shifts are very disturbing because they represent a deep decline in our moral character and our capacity for compassion. As a society, we are more concerned with ourselves—our individual wealth and our personal comfort— and less concerned with the less fortunate. We are preoccupied with material things and less occupied with spiritual things. Our borders are broken, our educational system lags behind those of other developed countries, our political system is corrupted with self-centered, greedy, and in many cases unethical politicians who think only of themselves and the special-interest groups they claim they do not represent. Our infrastructure is collapsing around us. We need a special Super Committee specifically formed to address these societal issues and to craft policies that will in effect put President Kennedy's words into action: "Ask not what your country can do for you—ask what you can do for your country." It is about time we took a trip back to the old America, where people were self-reliant, where hard work, dedication, and commitment meant something very special and we taught our children those values. An America where we respected one another and would go out of our way to help others in need. I strongly believe that this is what President Kennedy was asking of us as citizens. All of these values and behaviors are possible if you believe in them and expect your children to model them in daily interactions throughout their lives.

As our culture has shifted in negative ways, so has our sense of personal responsibility and accountability, to the detriment of society. Regarding personal responsibility and accountability, the changes we have experienced over the past sixty years have been extremely negative in their influence on our national culture. Actually, a lack of personal responsibility exists everywhere in our society and does not skip any socioeconomic group. It exists throughout our government; no individual or group of individuals, regardless of political affiliation, will take responsibility for the current state of affairs regarding our economic situation, energy crisis, educational failure, level of unemployment, or the exploding amount of our national debt. After four years of President Obama's administration being in power, some of the so-called best and brightest politicians are still blaming President Bush for all of the issues we are facing as a nation. There comes a point in every administration when the president needs to step forward and accept ownership of the problems and proactively initiate the necessary policies and decisions that will correct the problems. He cannot become so occupied with his reelection or influenced by special-interest groups that he continues to blame someone else. He needs to stand on his own two feet and say, I am responsible and I will fix these issues.

For example, our educational system is broken. We rank number one or two in the world regarding the amount of money spent per student, yet in math and science our students do not even rank in the top twenty developed countries. There are a lot of fingers being pointed at a lot of different groups, but nobody has accepted responsibility for the decline and nobody has put forth strategies to fix the problem. However, you only need to look back at the educational reforms that took place in the '60s and '70s, coupled with the decline in our moral values and the increasing power of our teachers' union, to start to understand why our educational system is not working. No personal responsibility means no ownership of the problem. No ownership of the problem means no motivation or courage to fix the problem. No motivation or courage to fix the problem makes it very easy to blame someone else.

Let's take a moment to look at the individual citizens. Our society has become lawsuit crazy. Whether I burned my mouth on a hot pickle on my Big Mac or I gained weight eating Big Macs, I am going to sue you because it is your fault, not my fault. This craziness to sue anyone for anything has gotten way out of control. The threat of lawsuits has forced many good doctors to give up their medical practice. It has caused many small business owners to say enough is enough and close up their shops. It has forced the medical community to perform unnecessary diagnostic medical procedures and tests just to protect themselves from the possibility of lawsuits. This situation drives up the cost of health care for everyone.

Businesses have had to add an inordinate amount of stickers, labels, and tags to their products to remind us not to put our kids in the oven, dryer, washing machine, or microwave. Your mattress and pillows come with tags that you had better not remove under penalty of law. You slip, you sue. If you burglarize a home and you get shot or beaten up, you sue the homeowners because of duress and psychological damage that you, the perpetrator of the crime, have experienced. Your kids become overweight and you sue the fast-food restaurant. Your kids receive bad grades in school and you blame the teachers. It could not be the fact that little Jonnie and Janie spent their time playing video games or texting their friends when they should have been at the library studying.

There is another dynamic at play here, and the finger of guilt is pointing in the direction of the liberalization of America. Nobody is personally responsible for anything that happens in his or her life. It is always someone else's fault. People say that they have no control over what happens to them. It is the big corporation, the teacher, the cop, the manager, the store clerk who caused the problem. It is never me. In behavioral psychology, people with this type of thinking and approach to life are said to have an *external locus of control*; they do not believe that they can control events and situations that they encounter in their lives. What we need is a nation of people who demonstrate an *internal locus of control*. That is, people who say, I am responsible for what happens in my life. I can influence, to a certain degree, the events and situations that I will encounter in my life's journey. I can proactively solve problems and address issues and challenges I will face in my life. I will not blame others; I will look to myself and see what I can do to correct the situation, right the wrong, or fix the problem. I am the keeper of my destiny. I will not rely on others for my future success. I will create my own future success. I am captain of my life's ship. Let's stop the lawsuits and let's start to fix the problems. The one great thing about religion and personal responsibility is that it does not matter if you are Muslin, Jewish, Christian, Hindu, or Buddhist; your religion will ask you to be accountable for your words and deeds, your behavior and attitude. Your religion asks you to stand before your God and say, "I have lived my life according to your teachings. I have cared about my fellow man, and I have taken responsibility for my life's choices."

I understand that there needs to be a separation of church and state, but I also believe that there would be a significant increase in personal responsibility and accountability if we did not neuter our educational system of its ability to embrace and demonstrate more of the values associated with religious teachings and spirituality. Again, there should be room for everyone's God in our culture.

Let's summarize the trends that are degrading American culture and destroying our moral compass.

- The infiltration of inappropriate language and behavior through the various forms of media and entertainment venues.

- The purging of anything religious from our daily lives, and that includes a full-blown assault on our traditions and holidays.

- The advancement of permissive behavior and overt, sexually explicit behavior in our movies, media, radio, and TV shows.

- The loss of the concept of personal responsibility for one's actions, words, and deeds.

- The liberalization of our educational system to where the focus is not on teaching the student but on the bureaucracy and personal power of the administration, teacher unions, and government.

- The loss of a sense of community and what it means to help others.

- The focus on "what is in it for me" versus "how can we all succeed."

- A tendency to sue rather than to say, I understand, I can forgive, it's not your fault.

Another major force influencing and shaping our culture is technology, including social media. Fifty years ago, you did not have personal computers, cell phones, smartphones, video games, Facebook, Twitter, or cable TV. The newspaper was your prime source of information, supported by the big three TV network news organizations, ABC, CBS, and NBC. There was no satellite reporting, no Skype from the field, no instant messaging. You would wait for the Sunday paper to get more in-depth analysis of what was happening in the world and, for that matter, your local community. Today you get instant analysis of current events as they unfold. We have access to a wide variety of 24/7 cable networks as well as an endless amount of information on the Internet. Via these media, you can actually witness events happening right in front of your eyes. This explosion of information is shaping current events. You can create a mob scene and riot at a shopping mall just by communicating to your friends on your smartphone via Facebook or Twitter. Every event is now captured on someone's cell phone and pictures uploaded to the Internet immediately. There are very few places in some of our big cities where you are not being watched by the eye of some camera.

This new technology has had an enormous positive impact on our lives. Technology has been used to drastically improve health care and to deliver alternative forms of education, training, and learning in general, as well as banking, shopping, travel, entertainment, and communications. Virtually every aspect of our lives has been touched in some way by these new technologies. Some people can even attend church services at home via their computer. However, any new technology can be abused if it is used inappropriately. Some of these abuses involve the Internet. The number one issue is the accessibility of pornography. The perverse and disgusting lowlifes not just in our society but throughout the world are using the Internet to sell pornography and sexually perverse materials, and there is little we can do about it. You can put software on your computer to filter out undesirable websites, but that protects your kids only while they are home. There was a recent story on one of the major news stations where they caught on videotape men at a public library watching graphic pornographic videos on the library's computers while children were sitting next to them doing their homework and researching school projects. If you happen to be looking up a web address and enter the wrong spelling in your Google search box you might pull up a porn site. We must do something about this situation to protect our children. When the Founding Fathers put pen to paper to write our First Amendment to give all of our citizen's freedom of speech, they never could have imagined anything like this. They could not have envisioned the technology we use today as our standard means of communicating. In addition, this perversion has enslaved little children in the sex trade for the pleasure of self-centered adults. Women and children mean nothing to these sick individuals. You may not like it, but we must ban access to this filth and perversion on any public computer or device. If it is okay to ban God from our society, why can't we ban and prosecute the perverts who make this obscenity, and send to prison anyone who uses children in these materials? The United Nations must get tougher with sex trafficking throughout the world, especially when it involves children and kidnapped women.

To close this chapter I am going to include a summary from *Death of the American Heart* regarding values and culture that will underscore my point that we have experienced a major negative shift in our national culture.

"Many of our citizens have lost their ability to respect others and their property. They have put themselves in the front of the line for self-satisfaction. It is all about them, their needs, their wants, their desires, their careers, their comfort, and they have no compassion for others. It is so sad to see our once-great citizens go from barn raising to barn busting. To go from compassionate and caring neighbors to critical and condescending people who cast a dark shadow onto others. To go from people who are walking in the path of light, next to God, to people walking in the shadow of evil. We are transforming from a society of individuals who want to do good deeds for others to one of individuals who are driven by greed and engage in deeds of dishonor against others. Wouldn't it be nice if every one of our citizens did one good deed a day to help someone less fortunate? Those acts of kindness would create a blanket of goodness over our great society. They would create a positive energy force, a feeling of purpose and meaning. The veil of negativity that covers our country would be lifted. A warm and caring feeling toward everyone, regardless of their situations, would be present within all of our actions and institutions. Christians, Jews, Muslims, and Atheists would be living and working together, guided by our core values and principles. All people would not only be tolerated but also respected and included.

To continue to explore the dynamics of our citizens and social system, I would like to reacquaint you with the hard face of reality, that a good number of our children are being raised in an environment of poverty and crime, in dysfunctional families that often lack a good male role model. Our prison system is overflowing with black and Hispanic young men and women. The large majority of those men and women were kissed with the curse of a perpetuating cycle of hopelessness, despair, and few opportunities, except those offered by a life of crime on the streets. These young people are destined to follow a path that will lead to prison or an early death:

- *Their parents have failed them.*

- *The educational system has failed them.*

- *The business community has failed them.*

- *The government has failed them.*

- *Society in general has failed them.*

- *And they have failed themselves.*

A good percentage of them were born into dysfunctional families. Many were born to teenage mothers and had no fathers in their lives. They have grown up in neighborhoods filled with crime, drugs, and alcohol abuse. They have not been taught the social graces or values necessary to become productive members of society. Instead, their values are those of the street. They are broken with despair, enraged with envy, and their lives are darkened by loneliness from a lack of love. They have been embraced by an undesirable element in our society. They are overwhelmed by fear, and it gives them no quarter. Whether at home, in school, or on the playground, fear is always watching over them. Their hearts have been hardened by a lack of success and recognition. They not only envy society, but loathe it. Stealing is their reward in life. Drugs are what comfort their soul. By the time they realize that in fact there are opportunities for them, it is too late. The train of life has left them in the station of despair.

This is our greatest social (cultural) problem to solve, and it is solvable. The answer is a very simple one; the application of the answer is almost impossible. To believe it can be solved, you must think that the impossible is possible, that the unthinkable is doable, and that every one of our children has the capacity for success and the opportunity for a life of enjoyment and satisfaction.

The following is my simple but almost impossible solution:

- The creation and assimilation of a strong set of family values into all aspects of our culture.

- The development of excellent pre-K-through-twelfth-grade educational systems, the best in the world.

- The guarantee of a good job, with businesses and corporations locating offices and plants within our most disadvantaged cities and towns.

- A judicial system that is just and rehabilitative in nature.

To break the cycle of despair and darkness, we need to reestablish a strong sense of family and a traditional set of values. The government, community leaders, business leaders, and school officials can all play a major role in turning the situation around. We can invest in our inner cities. We can, if we choose, reengineer our schools. Finally, rather than sending jobs to China and India, we could send them to our poorest cities and towns, thereby raising the standard of living for the most deserving of our citizens.

The greatness of a nation is measured by the heart and soul of its people:

- The compassion and caring they exhibit toward their fellow citizens.

- The respect they show for the property of others.

- Their dedication to country and community.

- Their demonstration of behaviors and deeds that show they are proud to be American.

- The honesty and truthfulness they manifest as they go about living their lives.

- Their commitment to the values and ideals of this great nation.

- Their willingness to sacrifice for the betterment of their fellow citizens.

- Their modeling of the teachings of their religions.

- Their belief that their word is their bond.

- Their love of country and the American dream.

- Their commitment to education and hard work.

- Their belief that we are a great nation sustained by the tapestry of exceptional people.

This is how we should conduct our lives as Americans.

So, how does the negative shift in the American culture impact Congress and the actions of the Super Committee? The culture of demonstrating a lack of personal responsibility and accountability directly influences the behavior of members of Congress and certainly impacts the behavior of members of the Super Committee. It provides cover under the security blanket of blame. Each political party blames the other party for the inability of the Super Committee to compromise on critical areas such as tax (increases versus no increases) and cuts to certain entitlement programs (cuts versus no cuts). Each party creates its own escape route and blames the other party for the Super Committee's inability to make the necessary tough choices required to bring about fiscal stability. A culture of lack of personal responsibility makes it very easy to step back and throw stones of disrespect. It makes it easy to mask yourself and your political party with the illusion of truth, while laying the blame squarely at the feet of the other party.

It makes it very easy to manipulate politically gullible constituents who believe that nothing will happen. Actually, the constituents have been brainwashed from the beginning not to expect anything positive because the other party will not compromise because of pressure from their special-interest groups and their core ideology. Therefore, the Super Committee actually failed before it held its first meeting.

Congress and the president and his cabinet heads, as well as our business leaders, need to look into their souls and say to themselves, "I need to compromise, to think and act in the best interests of the American people. I am willing to sacrifice, to right our great ship of state."

Chapter # 4

The Current State of Our Political System

The best way to describe the current state of our political system is to classify it as dysfunctional and out of control. I do not see any significant movement toward reforms that will bring the changes necessary to reduce the bureaucracy, control spending, realign the federal government with its constitutional mandates, and eliminate programs and services that do not support those constitutional mandates or add value to our nation, citizens, or states.

If we take a look at what has been going on with the various presidential races over the past fifteen years and what is going on in this election cycle, the average American citizen would come to the conclusion that our democratic system of government is broken. To help put this issue of a dysfunctional governmental process into an appropriate context, I will use some excerpts from my first book, *Death of the American Heart*, and I will add some updated observations to support my opinions. The 2008 election process for the presidency of the United States took over two years to select the Republican and Democratic presidential candidates and to elect Barack Obama as our forty-fourth president. Some politicians and potential candidates continued to position themselves for the 2012 race. They never stopped running, and some new presidential hopefuls jumped in and began testing the waters without delay.

What transpired during the 2008 presidential race and what continues to be the acceptable norm of behavior for both parties represents a microcosm of how our political system works. It pains me to state that the system does not work. It seems to be perfectly acceptable for candidates on both sides of the political spectrum to use deception when presenting their point of view, to take the other candidates' statements and distort them, to use their competitors' sound bites to portray them in an unfavorable light, and to allow their own political action groups to wage a negative advertising campaign against their rivals in a scorched-earth approach. It has been okay to attack another candidate's family and to go back more than twenty years to focus on a specific section of a speech the other candidate made, in an effort to discredit that person in the eyes of the voting public. Just recently, Mitt Romney's wife was attacked by a Democratic Party strategist who stated that Mrs. Romney has never worked a day in her life. This was not just an insult against Mrs. Romney but an insult to every woman who stayed home to raise a family. Mrs. Romney raised five sons, and I would consider that incredibly hard work. I can speak with authority on this subject because my daughter, Aimee, has four boys and one girl. She is constantly busy with her kids' activities and schoolwork. What arrogance this Democratic Party strategist showed. This is just the type of disrespectful behavior I am referring to when I said that some people are attacking not only the candidates but also their family members. I do not care that President Obama ate dog, nor do I care about Mitt Romney putting his dog on the top of his car and driving to a vacation spot. What I personally care about is creating good jobs, improving our educational system for our children, creating a good and affordable health care system for all Americans, reducing our national debt, fixing our government, and stopping the insanity of outsourcing our jobs to China and India. What Mitt Romney did forty-eight years ago in high school or what President Obama did in college is not relevant to our sustainable success as a nation. Politics today is a negative process: instead of focusing on the excessive debt we are accumulating as a result of out-of-control spending by Congress, our Republican and Democratic politicians spend their time trying to discredit the other party and pushing their own party's myopically focused agenda. Both parties should be willing to compromise and work together in the best interests of the country. The behavior in Washington is not about acting in the best interests of the American people, however; it is about acting in the best interests of the various special-interest groups that support one's party.

Instead of focusing on the slow economy, the outrageous gas prices, the decline of our middle class, the high unemployment rate, the loss of our manufacturing base, the erosion of our global leadership, and the poor performance of our educational system, our politicians instead focus on how they can destroy the other party, gain additional power, support their special-interest groups, and become personally wealthy in the process. The bottom line is that we have a dysfunctional government influenced more by the rich and powerful Washington lobbyists and elite groups than by the average American citizens. Average American citizens live by the rules, work hard, and try to do the best they can to raise their families and support their communities and churches, while trying to catch a little bit of the American dream. They pay their taxes and various government fees. All they expect is a fair wage and a sense of security. They vote to send their elected officials to Washington to represent their current interests and the future welfare of their children. They think that these officials will look out for them and the country, and that they will abide by the constitution, behave in a moral way, try to remove obstacles, and support an American vision of greatness and leadership in the world.

So what really happens? The people we elect, either Republican or Democrat, arrive in Washington and are assimilated into a code of conduct that is adversarial toward the opposing political party. The cancer of greed, the quest for power and influence, and self-interested behavior infect the Washington, DC, operating culture. Our elected officials are coerced by the established political brokers, incentivized by committee appointments and earmark bribes. The people we elect to represent us lose their ability to think on their own. They don't make decisions in the best interests of the country and of their states, but lose their souls to the greed of opportunity. This corruption of thought is tearing away at the heart of our country and the constitutional rights given to us by our Founding Fathers.

Our congressional officials are harassed by a deluge of special-interest groups and highly paid lobbyists who only want to advance their niche agendas even at great cost to the American people and our national treasure. Many of our elected officials and cabinet executives forget that they are supposed to represent the citizens of the United States and have been given the opportunity by the citizens to serve in the best interests of the country and their state. Instead of embracing and doing what is right for the country, many of our politicians start to operate in the best interests of their political party and the hundreds of special-interest groups and lobbyists that contribute to their election campaigns. Many of our Washington officials are driven by greed and power, and they become corrupt and unable to make the right but tough decisions. All you need to do is measure the success, or should I say lack of success, of the Super Committee. When our nation needed leaders the most, these committee members cowered in the shadows of their political party's self-interest and demonstrated a lack of courage. This gutless act, perpetrated on the American people, demonstrates a great disrespect for the soul of our country. Many of our Washington officials have lied to and cheated the very country and constituency they are supposed to represent.

This type of inappropriate behavior and failure to exercise the fortitude, courage, and leadership to do what is right for the nation has accelerated the current spending orgies and pork-barrel projects, where our political leaders embrace legislation suggested or advanced by powerful lobbyists and Washington insiders. These corrupt and arrogant politicians continue to demonstrate a lack of concern for America and the American worker. Our best and brightest political leaders have created a bloated, ineffective, non-value-added bureaucratic government that continues to fund programs that do not make any sense and that do not add value to the American way of life. The Washington politicians and the various departments pass laws and create policies and regulations that put us at a competitive disadvantage in the global marketplace. They make it difficult for small businesses to grow and expand. They develop pages and pages of forms to be completed by our citizens; they make the simple, complicated and the complicated, impossible. There is no sense of service to the American citizen, no sense of fairness, no accountability on the part of our government officials or government employees, no commitment to provide an excellent level of customer service to our citizens. Yet, they can mock the taxpayer, as the employees of the General Accounting Office did in an off-site team-building meeting in Las Vegas, where they produced mocking skits while they partied and spent nearly a million dollars on the retreat. They even gave some General Services Administration employees bonuses for organizing such a successful meeting. I guess in Washington, DC, success is measured by how much of the taxpayers' money you can waste on frivolous projects.

However, the problems I have described above are not the really big ones. The most significant problem that our elected officials and their surrogates perpetuate is simply their inability to engage in healthy and constructive debate, discourse, or disagreements without ugly attacks on other individuals or political parties. During the 2008 and 2012 presidential campaigns the candidates were on every major cable news network as well as the key TV shows on the big three networks, on radio, and in the print media. The following is a summary of what I personally saw and heard:

- The majority of the candidates and their surrogates distorted the position of the opposing candidates with a constant stream of lies, half-truths, and misrepresentations. These individuals were able to polarize the American voters with a senseless diatribe of lies and misstated facts.

- The candidates constantly made false assumptions and took out of context what the other candidate had said. They then put a negative spin on what the other candidate had said or done, or what they stood for.

- Quite a few candidates, their surrogates, or representatives of their PACs operated with mean, hateful, and dishonest intentions. A few stooped very low to hurt the other candidates and even went after their family members.

- With great indignation, arrogance, and uncontrolled egos, these individuals engaged in a scorched-earth approach to destroy the other candidates and their political parties.

- Many of the major media outlets, which are supposed to remain neutral, failed to maintain their objectivity and engaged in perpetuating these politically polarizing behaviors.

A classic example of this type of arrogance and complete disregard for the wishes of the American people perpetuated by the Democratic Party and the liberal media pundits was their reaction to citizens, especially members of the Tea Party, who protested the health care reform bill. These average American citizens were vilified and attacked by the same politicians they had elected to represent them. These politicians, supported by the liberal media, key members of Congress, and President Obama and his administration, accused these citizens of being unpatriotic, un-American, radical, and (by a few members) racist. In my view, these were loyal and decent Americans who just happened to disagree with the proposed health care legislation reform bill. Many of these patriotic Americans only wanted Congress to start over with a clean slate and include the voice of the people in the process. Many agreed that health care reform is necessary but wanted a slower and more thoughtful approach. Finally, some just wanted Congress and President Obama to read the 2,500-page bill to fully understand the consequences before they passed it. A few other groups wanted tort reform and a crackdown on the blatant Medicaid and Medicare fraud first, and then wanted to tackle the other areas of health care reform. And yes, a few wanted to kill the bill.

In trying to understand what happened, I ask myself the following questions: why was the voice of the majority of the American people disregarded? Why were these American citizens disrespected by their own government officials? Do we really not care about our middle-class and elderly Americans? They were not invited to the socialist buffet of greed, corruption, and excessive spending. What the average middle-class or elderly American experienced was a blatant abuse of power by our elected governmental officials and the Obama administration. Not only was the will of the majority of American citizens ignored—regarding their concerns and disagreements and their displeasure with the way the health care reform legislation was created— but our congressional leaders and White House officials verbally attacked those who opposed their decision as being radicals and un-American. As I stated previously, Speaker Pelosi went as far as to say we need to pass the bill so we can read the bill. Did you ever hear anything as stupid as that statement made by the Speaker of the House of Representatives? Pass the bill so we can read the bill. Why not read the bill to understand exactly what it contains before you pass it? The passage of the health care reform legislation just underscores the arrogance of some of our government officials.

Whatever happened to constructive political discourse and debate? I will answer that question. Simply, the Obama administration did not want a debate or public discussion forum on the health care reform bill because they did not want you to know what was actually in the bill. Get ready for hidden taxes, rationing, cutbacks in Medicare, incredible bureaucratic increases in paperwork, services being denied, and a massive degradation of our overall health care system. All of which will conveniently kick in after the 2012 presidential election is over. This was done so President Obama and his administration can postpone—until after he is reelected— the moment when you, the average American middle-class citizens, and you, our senior citizens, realize that you have just been screwed over by the Obama administration. So, folks, the election is over and it is now that you will be negatively impacted by the new health care legislation. It will be too late to change your vote to the Republican candidate. For those of you who want to sell your home after 2013, be prepared to pay a 3.8% tax, a fact which is buried in the 2,500-page bill. If you are elderly with serious medical conditions, be prepared to be denied services based on an economic formula. Some of you will have to pay for your own hip or knee replacement. Forget about a transplant, but get ready for comfort care. When you are denied services that will keep you alive for a few more years, I guess the decision-making body could be construed as a death panel of sorts. Comfort care for a few months versus medical procedures that will give you a few more years. What would you call it?

What is the solution to this quagmire of deceit, dishonesty, and unprofessional behavior? There is no simple answer, but a host of reforms, difficult decisions, and policy changes must be made to reengineer our government. First, we need to establish a strong third party, a Reagan Democratic-like party, founded on the principles and values that have made this a great country. The third-party candidate needs to be driven by a sense of duty, honor, and integrity, and a desire to serve our nation. We need a third party that will be willing to eliminate the staggering bureaucracy in Washington. A party that will streamline policies and procedures that currently inflict pain and suffering on many of our fellow citizens. We need a party we can trust and party members who demonstrate trustworthy behavior. We need a party with elected officials who will work in the best interests of the American people and not serve the interests of lobbyists or their particular personal agendas for acquiring power and wealth.

Next, we need term limits that eliminate the need for reelection campaigns. When we elect people to Congress for a two-year term, they basically never get out of their reelection mentality and they become susceptible to being held hostage by the special-interest groups and lobbyists who contributed to their campaigns. The following are some ideas for term limits:

- The president of the United States should be elected for one term of six years. If the president cannot achieve his or her agenda in six years, two more years will not matter. Senators should be elected for one term of six years. The election process could be phased in so that every two years, one-third of the Senate will change.

- Congressional representatives should be elected for one term of four years. This supports the intent of our Founding Fathers to send average citizens to Congress and then have them return to their communities. No more career politicians.

We should also reengineer the role of our federal government to bring it back into alignment with the vision of our Founding Fathers and the constitutional intent. This reengineering effort should include a complete review of all federal agencies and the various programs they support, to determine if they are absolutely necessary. If they are deemed not to be a mission-critical agency or program then they should immediately be eliminated.

Chapter # 5

Recommendations for Congress from
Death of the American Heart

The recommendations I have included in Chapter 1 represent my thoughts on what the Super Committee should have discussed during their strategic brainstorming and planning sessions. What I have included below are my key thoughts and recommendations that were contained in my first book, *Death of the American Heart*. I wanted the book to be prescriptive in its content and provide solutions that are doable. I have included them in this book to capture, in one place, all the recommendations that I have personally brainstormed and identified as potential solutions to some of the political, social, and financial challenges facing our nation today. They may not all make sense to you, and certainly I do not expect you to agree with all of them. I have not vetted these ideas or empirically researched their applicability. However, they do represent the type of out-of-box thinking that needs to take place to change the paradigm in Washington, DC, and allow our political and business leaders to create the bold reforms and changes necessary to transform our nation back to a state of greatness.

If I were in Congress, these are the types of recommendations I would put forth on the floor of the Senate or within the halls of Congress. They are innovative and thought provoking, and they represent the type of robust changes that we need to make, as a country, to get back on a fiscally responsible track. Yes, some of them are very controversial, but we need to treat our country with a radical surgical procedure because as a country, we are very sick. We do not need incremental changes, but instead we need radical change and transformation; I offer what I believe are viable solutions to many of our political, financial, and social problems. The following are ideas and recommendations from *Death of the American Heart*:

Quoting from my first book, I would like to take a moment to review what I consider to be some of the most significant recommendations that will help to transform our nation to a state of greatness once again. If we embrace and implement these recommendations, and if we honor the spirit of our Founding Fathers, our Constitution, the Bill of Rights, and our moral heritage, we will once more be the leader in the free world and keeper of the light of liberty. My overarching recommendations are as follows:

- The president of the United States and Congress shall create a new national vision for America that will act as the engine for change and transformation, allowing our nation to once again achieve a state of greatness like the one that President Kennedy created in the '60s. Through President Kennedy's vision of putting a man on the moon, he put America in first place as the greatest nation that ever existed. The ball rests in the president's court to craft such a vision and have Congress approve it as the driving force and beacon of light as our nation aspires to achieve its goals.

- The president of the United States and Congress should create a core set of shared national values that will permeate every corner of our society and touch every citizen. These shared values should be reflected in the behavior of all American citizens, regardless of age, profession, economic status, religion, or political affiliation. These values should be reflected in all policies and laws that are developed by our federal, state, and local governments.

- Businesses and organizations of all types will need to embrace these shared values in their interactions with clients, customers, consumers, employees, business partners, suppliers, key stakeholders, and constituents.

- Schools, colleges, and universities must create institutions that support, reflect, and reinforce these shared values as they go about the business of educating our children, young men and women, and future leaders of our nation. Values, ethics, and personal integrity should be included in the core-teaching curriculum for all grade levels.

- We must maintain our traditions and holidays as a nation, and be tolerant and supportive of the cultural diversity and unique traditions of the various groups that represent the tapestry of our citizenry.

- We should be able to make room for the various gods our citizens worship as we pursue our national vision. There should always be room for one's god on our journey to sustained greatness as a world leader.

- The president of the United States and Congress must develop a set of strategies that will rebuild our manufacturing base. These strategies should include the creation of a tax policy that will help attract manufacturing back to the United States and is business-friendly.

- Enterprise manufacturing "no tax" zones should be established in the hundred most impoverished communities in the United States. Extra tax incentives should be given to any company that returns to the United States the manufacture of products and the operation of services that were previously outsourced to offshore vendors.

- The president of the United States and Congress should create a law requiring that the budget be balanced. No deficit spending should be allowed. This law should also mandate a "one item, one bill" requirement. No more pork or add-on projects should be allowed. Each appropriation should stand on its own merits.

- There should be mandatory prison sentences for politicians, lobbyists, and business leaders doing business with the government who are convicted of corruption. These convicted individuals should serve hard time—no more country-club prisons.

- Congress should rewrite the tax code to be a flat tax for both individuals and businesses—no more special deductions. You make X, you pay Y—no more writing off your vacation home, boat, trips, etc.

- Utilizing the available technology, we should downsize the federal government by at least 30 percent. We should reengineer every federal agency and eliminate those that do not add value anymore, are redundant, or do not meet the means test for being critical to the core mission and purpose of the federal government. We should shift as many services as possible to Internet transactions.

- We should immediately reengineer our kindergarten-through-twelfth-grade educational systems. We should start by significantly reducing the bureaucracy of the US Department of Education and recharter the agency with creating the necessary protocols, policies, and actions that will position our children as the most educated in the world, with top rankings in math, science, and technology. This redesign should include the creation of a two-track system, one track being academically oriented and the other technology oriented. The technology track should include studies in green technology, biotechnology, computer technology, chemistry, physics, and science.

- As soon as our children are toilet trained, we should start their basic educational process, which will include a foundation in reading, math, science, technology, and a foreign language.

- The US Department of Education should be downsized and the freed-up assets reallocated to the states for the purpose of creating centers of educational excellence, especially in high-crime, high-poverty, and high-dropout areas.

- To be eligible for the reallocated funds, each state must reduce the ratio of administrative personnel to teachers.

Each senior-level administrative person must teach one class per semester.

- In addition to stimulating the minds of our children, we should also work on building physically fit and healthy students at all grade levels. Physical activity and good nutrition should be built into the curriculum at all grade levels.

- The school day should be lengthened to match that of other nations with which we are competing in the global marketplace. This will also allow our schools to develop intramural sports programs in which all students must participate during the school week.

- Teachers must participate in mandatory training each year that meets specific knowledge standards, and they should receive performance evaluations based on results. If they don't meet the knowledge standards and their classroom performance is below par, they should be put on a developmental plan to correct their performance. After one semester, if they have not improved their performance, they should be placed on developmental probation designed to increase their level of competence. If after two full school years their performance has not improved substantially, they should be terminated.

- We should immediately issue a mandate for the United Nations to reform and eliminate corruption. The UN should be required to restructure itself to become more effective and efficient. Just like our federal government, the United Nations must conduct an agency-by-agency performance review and eliminate any agency or part thereof that is not adding value to the citizens of the world. The United States should start to reduce its contribution to the UN by 20 percent per year if there are no substantial signs of reform.

- Congress should pass laws that are aimed at reforming our legal system. Strong tort reform should be mandated, with the goals of eliminating frivolous lawsuits, streamlining our judicial process, capping damages awarded, and placing accountability for one's personal actions in the process. Medical malpractice laws should be established to bring fairness and sensibility into the process, which will not adversely affect good doctors.

- Stiff, swift, and mandatory penalties should be established to curb the Medicare and Medicaid fraud that is currently rampant in the system. Violators should be sent to jail quickly. The government needs to redirect some assets from other agencies to identify the most corrupted areas of the country, and with a SWAT-like mentality make the necessary interventions to put the cheats in jail.

- We need to restructure how we provide foreign aid to other countries. We should place a moratorium on all financial foreign aid for a two-year period. No money should be given to any country during this time. Instead of providing money during these two years, we will continue to provide food, medicine, and technical support as needed, but financial payments should stop. During this period, we should profile the needs of our own country regarding roads, bridges, light rail, hospitals, and school upgrades, and allocate some of these earmarked foreign-aid funds to improve our own infrastructure. We will not give money to dictators and government leaders who oppress, torture, or disrespect their citizens. Instead, we will use other channels to provide food, medicine, and infrastructure support.

- We must allow our traditions and holidays to be honored in all our facilities. We need to reverse the trend of being too politically correct and allow our children, for instance, to celebrate Christmas, Hanukkah, etc., in schools and other public places throughout our great land.

- Congress must create a law that prohibits add-ons and pork to bills. We need a "one item, one bill" law. Congress can create other mechanisms for dealing with special projects using the conference committee and subcommittee infrastructure. Major legislation must stand on its own and not be hijacked with pork spending projects as legally attached parasites.

- Congress and the president of the United States must maintain a balanced budget. No more deficit spending.

- The silent majority needs to become more active and form the basis for a viable third party.

- We are no longer at war with Germany or Japan, so why not close our foreign military bases? We could save tens of billions of dollars a year if we closed 50 percent of our bases overseas. All of this money could be allocated for education and enterprise manufacturing zones. The Cold War is over, and a new strategic defensive plan regarding global bases needs to be developed.

- We must stop trying to purge God and patriotism from the lives of our children. The framers of our Constitution identified the issues with the separation of church and state, but we have gone way too far in trying to be politically correct. Bring back school prayer and have our children not only say the Pledge of Allegiance to the flag, but sing "The Star-Spangled Banner" every day. We should make it okay to talk about the heroes of our past, and to honor and respect the men and women who wear our country's uniform.

Since I am proposing a new national vision, set of operating principles, shared values, and aspirations for our nation, I feel that I must clarify what they could possible look like and include. So, listed below is a proposed sample of the possibilities of what the vision, operating principles, and shared values might look like. I have also included a set of possible national aspirations. Our national vision, set of values, operating principles, and aspirations would be used as teaching and assimilation documents that will help reshape our society over the next several generations. They need to become part of the teaching curriculum from preschool right through college as well as reinforced within our business community and institutions. It is the only way we can shift our national culture back in alignment with our Founding Fathers moral compass.

A Potential National Vision

The United States of America will strive to become the most compassionate, caring, and supportive nation in the world. Our citizens will be the most educated workforce on the planet and will dedicate themselves to improving the quality of life for all humankind. We will lead the world in the development of technology. Whether it is medicine, food, clean water, energy, science, or transportation, we will develop and deploy these technologies throughout the world.

A Recommended Set of National Global Operating Principles

In our dealing with other nations, we will:

- Teach and not tell

- Counsel and not criticize

- Value and not vanquish

- Support and not scold

- Respect diversity and not try to force compliance

- Lead and not manage

- Promote a hand and not a handout

- Be forthright and honest and not deceiving

- Earn respect and not command respect

- Help and not forget

- Cure and not confuse

- Feed and not ignore

- Tolerate and not condemn

- Cherish and not control

- Love and not hate

A Possible set of National Core Shared Values

It is very important for me to clarify what I mean by a set of national core values. I can hear the critics now, saying, "How dare he recommend a set of values? Who does he think he is? Whose values are they, and what if I don't agree with these values?" I ask you to hold off on your judgment and criticism of my belief that we need to embrace and constantly reinforce a set of national core values that are taught from the day our children are born to the day they die. So please open your mind to at least exploring these values in the context of where our nation is currently—how Americans are living their lives and conducting themselves at work and in society. For every value that I list, there are thousands of Americans who are living those values every day and just as many fellow citizens who are not. I will first list the core values that I believe will strengthen the cultural fabric of our great nation if they are taught and constantly reinforced at home and throughout our school system. Second, I will add some additional context which I will import from *Death of the American Heart.*

The following are the core values I believe should be part of the American cultural fabric:

- **Respect**

- **Loyalty**

- **Honesty**

- **Integrity**

- **Hard work**

- **Dedication**

- **Commitment**

- **Sharing**

- **Helping others**

- **Compassion and caring**

- **Personal responsibility**

It is my strong belief that if there were more emphasis in our country on values, religion, and the various gods that represents the major religions, there would be a profound and positive impact on the behavior of future generations of adults in the United States. I also believe that teenage pregnancy would decline significantly and high school dropout rates, especially those of our minority students, would fall rapidly. Personal integrity and honesty would reassert itself in our academic, government, and business communities and relationships. I deeply believe that there would be a greater appreciation of diversity, a more willing attitude to help others in need, and an increased kindness to others, regardless of their lots in life or their backgrounds. In the long term, I think we would see a significant reduction of corruption among our government officials and business leaders.

For people who do not believe in God or have no affiliation with a religion, this is not a problem, because the values that our Founding Fathers espoused and the values I have listed above are universal in their association to all of humankind, and they apply to everyone in our country.

- Wouldn't you like to see the prison population in the United States decrease, especially the number of black and Hispanic young men?

- Wouldn't you like to see our elected representatives demonstrate a higher order of personal integrity?

- Wouldn't you like to see our business leaders and union leaders operate with a greater amount of openness and honesty in their transactions?

- Wouldn't it be great if our entertainers and sports heroes were outstanding role models for our youth to emulate?

- Wouldn't it be great to know that our young men and women embodied truth and decency in their interactions?

All of these things are possible if we embrace a value-driven philosophy throughout our society. A society that does not embrace a set of core operating principles will produce a society of misfits and socially irresponsible, self-centered, greedy, uncaring citizens. How could you argue that the values listed above are not an appropriate way to behave and conduct your life?

These values are the basic core elements of how we should treat each other, regardless of whether we believe in a God, Mother Nature, some other force in the universe, or just ourselves. If you disagree with these universal values, then what will you espouse as your central theme in life regarding how you behave, treat others, and function in our society? What would your values look like?

- If you could not embrace respect, would you be disrespectful to others?

- If you could not demonstrate loyalty, would you be disloyal to your family, friends, and employer?

- If you could not embrace honesty, would you lie and cheat your way through life?

- If you could not model integrity, would you allow yourself to engage in inappropriate behavior?

- If you could not work hard but are capable, would you be a slacker and have others pull your share?

- If you could not be dedicated, would you go through life without a purpose and sense of meaning?

- If you could not exercise commitment, would your word and handshake mean nothing in life's transactions?

- If you could not share, would you hoard and only take but never give of yourself?

- If you would not help others, would you become consumed with satisfying yourself and your personal needs and give nothing back to society?

- If you could not embrace compassion and caring for others, would you be so narcissistic that you thought only of your own comfort, wealth, power, and status?

- If you could not assume personal responsibility for your actions, words, and deeds, would you go through life blaming everyone else for your shortcomings, failures, and mistakes?

These are not the values of any one particular religion; instead they represent universal values that frame how people should treat others and conduct their lives on this earth. These are the values that need to be reinforced in our schools, religious institutions, businesses, and government organizations, and generally throughout the core of our society.

I hope that the above descriptions put in context how important values are in shaping our nation's culture. They must be articulated and reinforced throughout our educational system, business community, and public institutions to have a positive shaping effect on our culture and society.

Finally, I would like the president and members of Congress to consider what I call a national set of aspirations that are derived from our vision, operating principles, and core values. These are higher-level goals or results of our new national focus.

Potential List of National Aspirations

In our future society, our vision, operating principles, and core values will allow us to

- Educate everyone

- Feed the hungry

- Help the poor

- Cure the sick

- Eliminate crime as we know it

- Establish values throughout the land

- Be guided by morality

- Be honest in all our dealings

- Fix the systems that serve our citizens

- Provide good jobs for everyone

- Raise our standard of living

- Become exceptional stewards of the environment

As you can gather from reading this chapter, there is a lot of overlap and redundancy when it comes to potential solutions to our nation's most serious problems. This is important in my eyes because it solidifies many recommendations as having substantial merit, at least enough merit to engender a conversation. However, because of the current polarization of our two political parties and the pressures from special-interest groups, these recommendations will never reach the floor of Congress for debate unless you, the reader, create your own list of things you think need to change and send that to the Super Committee, the president, and your congressional representatives. In addition, I have one other simple request: please identify the recommendations or solutions that you believe would make a difference in helping our nation solve some of its major challenges, and use the power of your social network to communicate these solutions to your network contacts and your congressional representatives. We can use the power of the web and social networking to apply pressure on Congress to get serious about reforms before it is too late and we yield our global economic and technical leadership to China and India.

If you get involved and get your social network involved, it will be possible to once again develop a society of people who care for one another and are willing to help advance the standard of living and the quality of life for all Americans. We can, and I believe we will, continue to create the greatest society on the planet—if we embrace the necessary reforms to bring the pendulum back into the center of American life.

Chapter # 6

The Final Chapter

To summarize some disturbing societal trends, I would like to highlight a few situations and examples that are having an impact on the decline of our nation. The cost of medical coverage keeps going up, and yet the quality and level of service provided keeps on going down. Energy costs keep climbing without any explanation, yet we do not have a definite strategy to become energy independent. People don't take the time to be civil to each other or to care about their neighbors. It's a selfish state of mind. A large percentage of our population is looking for a free lunch:

- They are trying to get as much money and services from the government as they can with no regard to whether they need them or not.

- They are the citizen locusts of the twenty-first century.

- They are the "entitled," trying to beat the system, claiming that we owe them a living and they do not have to contribute anything in return.

- They gorge themselves at the trough that the government provides.

- In many cases they do not pay taxes or don't pay their fair share.

- They demand but are not tolerant.

- They take but will not give.

- They consume but will not help grow.

- They are self-absorbed but will not share.

- They demand respect but will not respect others.

- They do not tolerate criticism but will criticize others.

- For many people, God is dead and the power of the dollar rules.

- Sexuality has replaced spirituality.

- Insensitivity has replaced caring for others.

People are dying in this great nation because they cannot get adequate medical coverage. Children are going to bed hungry because they have not had access to food. We have parents that can't parent. We have fathers and mothers blinded by drugs and alcohol at the expense of their family's well-being. We have babies giving birth to babies, perpetuating the cycle of poverty and despair. We watch as some weekly television shows parade loser after loser on stage to discuss their personal problems, and we accept this level of degenerate behavior as part and parcel of our society. This is not how a great society operates. At the same time all this negative energy is eating away at the fabric of our way of life, a major assault on the middle class is taking place. Our middle-class family members have been downsized from their jobs or asked to do more with less pay, while executives get richer by outsourcing work to cheap labor markets overseas. Our middle class citizens have been overtaxed and underrepresented by their government. They have been cheated and abused by the health care system, and denied access to certain programs and benefits because of their savings and income levels. They continue to be exploited by the credit card companies, banks, and government officials that are supposed to have their best interests in mind. They are disrespected by the government that is supposed to care about them and protect them from harm. Our middle-class American families have been deeply harmed both financially and psychologically through the last four years of this economic and government meltdown.

I recognized that these negative trends were in play when I wrote the final chapter in my first book, and I listed twenty-one questions in the beginning of the final chapter, as a way of getting people to think about the current state of affairs of our nation. These questions acted to position the concepts in the final chapter as well as my concluding comments. They were specifically created to get the reader thinking about his or her particular situation. They were asked in the first part of the chapter to set the table for personal reflection and to create context for the reader to engage his or her family members and friends in a constructive dialogue. The questions are as follows:

1. Are you better off financially than you were ten years ago?

2. How has your 401(k) or retirement plan been performing? Have your assets lost value or gained value over the last few years?

3. How many family members, neighbors, acquaintances, or work colleagues do you know who have been adversely affected by outsourcing, downsizing, or globalization?

4. How has the value of your home been doing lately? Has it appreciated or declined during the past eight years?

5. How has your economic situation been doing lately? Have you received salary and merit increases commensurate with your performance and your contributions to the organization?

6. Do you and the other working members of your family feel more secure or less secure in your jobs than you did a few years ago?

7. Are you being asked to do more work, to work longer hours, and to be more flexible and open to change, and if so, are you being compensated for your increased level of work and commitment to the organization?

8. Do you feel that your elected officials are representing your interests more than they support special-interest groups?

9. Do you feel that middle-class American citizens are being fairly supported by our government and business leaders?

10. How is the mortgage foreclosure rate in your neighborhood? Is it acceptable?

11. How well are your local schools performing?

12. Is America becoming more moral or less moral, regarding the behavior of its citizens?

13. Are our citizens more caring or less caring for the disadvantaged among us? On the other hand, are they preoccupied with their own interests?

14. Does the global community care about our country and the well-being of our citizens and does it play fair and by the rules in the global competitive marketplace?

15. Is Congress more effective or less effective than it was ten years ago?

16. Do your children and grandchildren have a brighter future, a more secured future, and the opportunity for a higher standard of living than you had at their age?

17. Will the children born during the next ten years come into this world burdened by debt that an out-of-control Congress incurred during its watch?

18. Ten years from now, will America still be a leader in science, technology, medicine, food production, and manufacturing?

19. Will our military still be able to defend our nation and maintain its superpower status, ensuring that the forces of evil do not jeopardize the welfare of the world?

20. Will God, our traditions, values, and beliefs continue to be diminished in their ability to influence our moral behavior and culture?

21. Finally, will America continue to be the greatest nation that every occupied the planet or will we fade away into history's closet of civilizations that were once great but could not sustain their greatness? Will we survive?

Over the past several years, we have seen more layoffs due to outsourcing, more small businesses closed because of the economy, more home foreclosures, more homeowners who are upside-down on their mortgages (when the home value is less than the mortgage), more governmental dysfunction, and one of the worst recessions in our history. We have seen our kindergarten-through-twelfth-grade school system fall behind the top twenty countries in the world regarding our students' math and science scores. We have one of the worst high school dropout rates in the developed world. Our debt as a nation is consuming us and will sentence our children to incredible levels of taxation to pay it down. This debt has been fueled by a Congress that is out of control, with its frivolous spending and social welfare programs that we just cannot afford.

However, to get reelected our officials over-promise—to all their constituencies, big unions, and other special-interest groups—pieces of our national wealth that they do not deserve and that we cannot afford and, quite frankly, do not have without borrowing. We have given our manufacturing industry to China, we have sent our core information technology industry to India, we have given up our global leadership position in the world, we have downgraded our future by stripping from American citizens their hopes and dreams, and we have neutered our once-great military, putting our country and our citizens at great risk because we have failed to heed the words of President Theodore Roosevelt, who quoted the adage "speak softly but carry a big stick." We have not gone softly but instead have stumbled through the world's global issues. We have apologized to some of the bullies of the world for our past justifiable actions. We have put down our big stick, while China's stick is getting bigger and bigger and they continue to spy on us, cyber-attack our military infrastructure, and steal our jobs with cheap labor as a weapon. We cannot allow this lack of national leadership and widespread governmental incompetency to continue. We need to get all Americans thinking about the future of their children. If they do not, their children and their grandchildren will have a much lower standard of living than their own. We will also allow the bullies of the world to gain power and the perverted dictators of the world to continue to murder and torture their citizens. We will no longer be a great nation and civilization, but a nation on a steep decline with no real national vision or set of core principles and values. This lack of vision, values, and leadership has contributed to the current negative forces and trends. The gap has now become a chasm filled with negative energy and it continues to grow wider and deeper because we will not embrace the necessary changes nor make the necessary sacrifices as a country to reverse the trends. As a country, we need to embrace a set of principles and values based on respect, honesty, integrity, compassion, caring for our fellow Americans, and personal responsibility for our actions, words, and deeds. As a country, we continue to purge God and anything that has to do with religion from our society. That void is being filled by evil, disrespect, dishonesty, selfishness, and a genuine lack of compassion and caring. As more people look for a handout versus a helping hand, as they try to scam the system, as they continue to exploit their employers, neighbors, and shopkeepers, our society will crumble into a state of apathy and mediocrity. As we hurry about our daily lives, never once thinking about helping the less fortunate, we will become lonely and isolated. As we allow the most unfortunate of our society to continue to suffer in poverty, our children to go to bed hungry, our elderly citizens to endure the trials and tribulations of aging in places of loneliness, and our students to be denied a good education, we will have lost forever the vision of our Founding Fathers. Think about what we are doing to our children. We are condemning them to a life of misery and hopelessness. Future generations will not experience the great society that you and I have experienced. Future generations of Americans will not feel the greatness of our nation nor see its good work played out in the world raising the standard of living for the poor in the global community. We will have lost our global leadership in the league of nations and become a follower instead of a trailblazer.

These trends cannot continue or they will destroy our way of life as Americans. We cannot afford to ignore these conditions any more or our children will suffer immensely.

- We cannot afford another four years of political infighting, lack of courage, and lack of leadership on the part of the president and the leaders of both houses of Congress.

- We cannot afford to continue to destroy for another four years the future opportunities for our citizens by a government that is out of control.

- We cannot afford another four years of outsourcing our core manufacturing industries and our technology expertise to other countries.

- We cannot afford another four years of disrespecting our middle-class citizens and stealing their hopes and dreams.

- We cannot afford another four years traveling down the pathway to socialism.

- We cannot afford another four years in which our kindergarten-through-twelfth-grade students fall behind our global competitors.

- We cannot afford another four years of the moral decay, corruption, and greed that runs rampant through our various institutions.

- We cannot afford another four years of a government that does not work effectively.

- We cannot afford another four years of a tax structure that is unfair, overly complicated, and filled with loopholes, and that facilitates inequality.

- We cannot afford another four years of an onslaught of policies, rules, and regulations that are choking the innovative spirit and growth opportunities out of our small businesses.

- We cannot afford another four years of international nation building while our infrastructure crumbles.

- We cannot afford another four years of mounting debt and an unbalanced federal budget.

- We cannot afford another four years of complacently watching our nation fall behind India and China.

We *can* afford to make the necessary sacrifices to bring our nation back from the brink of disaster. We do not have a choice; it must be done, and you must become an instrument for creating a better America. In the next chapter, I will lay out some areas where you can directly implement the changes necessary to help America get back on the track to future success.

Chapter # 7

Actions We the People Need to Take

Is there hope for our great nation? The answer is unequivocally yes! There are tens of millions of great Americans yearning for change. They are the men, women, and children, old and young, who make up a tapestry of cultures, ethnicities, religions, and ideologies. They are what many have called the melting pot of our society. Some are new to our land, some have roots going back generations, and some have ancestral roots going back thousands of years. They all make up the human face of America, and they embrace and live under the constitutional philosophy of **"We the People."**

The Declaration of Independence clearly states the following:

We hold these truths to be self-evident, that all men are created equal, that they are endowed by their Creator with certain unalienable Rights, that among these are Life, Liberty and the pursuit of Happiness. — That to secure these rights, Governments are instituted among Men, deriving their just powers from the consent of the governed, — That whenever any Form of Government becomes destructive of these ends, it is the Right of the People to alter or to abolish it, and to institute new Government, laying its foundation on such principles and organizing its powers in such form, as to them shall seem most likely to affect their Safety and Happiness.

Our current government has become destructive because it is dysfunctional. Therefore, **We the People** have not only the right but the duty to change it.

- **We the People** deserve honest elected officials representing us. If it turns out that they are not living by a code of conduct that models the highest ethical standards possible, then we should vote them out of office and demand reforms that lead to integrity and accountability.

- **We the People** should band together in a quiet and peaceful revolution, using the power of our voices and the muscle of our votes to demand a balanced budget. No more pork. No more earmarks. No more backroom deals. No more putting the desires of special-interest groups over the needs of our citizens. No more personal agendas influenced by greed and dishonest behavior. We need to take back our government by the power of our united demonstrations.

- **We the People** need to take back our schools and start to create an educational system that will position our kindergarten-through-twelfth-grade students to be able to successfully compete with the best of their global counterparts. The ultimate goal should be for our children to be the most educated in the world or at least in the top three industrialized countries.

- **We the People** must say no to teacher unions and no to tenure for teachers who are inept. We should institute a performance-based model for all teachers and school administrative staff.

- **We the People** should demand reforms that lead to excellence in all our schools, no matter where they are located.

- **We the People** should dismantle the bureaucracy within our federal and state departments of education and create a new values-based science- and technology-driven educational system in all grade levels.

- **We the People** should demand that our traditions and values be honored and embraced in every classroom.

- **We the People** should expect that during a two- or four-year college degree program, significant emphasis is placed on ethics, integrity, and personal accountability.

- **We the People** should demand that, first and foremost, our business leaders think and act in the best interests of our nation. To lay off and destroy the lives of millions of American citizens so we can save a few dollars on products or make a few more dollars of profit is morally reprehensible. Given the right type of visionary leadership, we can reestablish a viable manufacturing industry in our country and once again demonstrate leadership and innovation. This requires vision and commitment on the part of our business leaders to invest in the necessary technologies, plants, and equipment that will allow us to competitively manufacture products in the United

States. It requires vision and commitment on the part of our political leaders to create tax, environmental, and regulatory policies friendly to business and in alignment with how other countries are supporting their manufacturing industries. It will require vision and commitment on the part of our union leaders to be reasonable in setting work rules that don't stifle creativity, innovation, and out-of-the-box thinking, as well as pay scales that don't force companies to outsource as their only alternative to reducing cost.

You can personally make a difference:

- Get involved.

- Run for office on a school committee or board.

- Vote out politicians who lack character and vote in politicians who demonstrate character and integrity.

- Don't buy products from companies that don't care about American workers.

- Say no to union greed.

- Demand reform in your schools, local government, and workplace.

- Don't settle for poor-quality products or services.

- Pay a little more and shop in stores that carry a balanced inventory of merchandise made in America and merchandise made overseas.

- Demand that our holidays and cultural traditions be honored in your local schools.

- Demand that teachers and administrators be held accountable for the performance of students and schools.

- Reinforce the values of family within your home.

- Establish and constantly reinforce a set of core values within your family and in youth groups or sports teams with which you are associated in your community.

- Volunteer, and go out of your way to help others in your community who are less fortunate.

- Do something nice for someone else every day. Make sure that everyone in your family does this. Small acts of kindness do matter and will amount to something very special.

- Don't sit back.

- Don't be quiet.

- Be passionate at work and look for opportunities to create positive change.

- As you become involved, say a prayer for the sick and dying, the poor and oppressed, and the lonely and starving people of the world.

Become an agent for positive change with your voice, with your vote, with your behavior, with your passion, with your heart, and with your soul. Embrace the core values of our heritage and model those values. Demonstrate your beliefs and principles in all aspects of your personal and professional life. Expect excellence from those who serve our citizens. Believe that you can make a difference to help create a better future for the next generation of Americans. You can become a Pilgrim, helping to establish new thinking paradigms that will reestablish the cultural fabric that will make us an exceptional nation of opportunity for all American citizens who want to taste success through their hard work and personal diligence. You will be helping to rekindle the American dream for many of our people. You can become a Patriot, ensuring that our constitutional freedoms live on and that our laws remain fair and just in their application. And yes, you can become a Pioneer, helping to create a vision and charting a new course that will lead to new frontiers of thought and behavior which will act as the framework for an ideal twenty-first-century America. Yes, you can, and yes, together we can make a profound difference in our destiny. There is no alternative road to our sustainable success as a nation. There is only one path to choose, and that path will lead us to the highway of success. This path represents the beacon of light that will energize our souls and guide us on our journey. For it is your destiny to make a difference in this wonderful country of ours.

To our friends in Congress, and to members of the Super Committee, the Tea Party, and the Occupy Wall Street movement: I encourage you to think about some of the ideas in this book plus your own ideas for saving our great nation. I implore you to engage in constructive debate and dialogue and to be willing to compromise in the best interests of our nation and it citizens. Please put on the back burner your personal ideological philosophy and embrace a new paradigm of thought and discussion. It is time for us to make the difficult decisions, it is time to discuss the undiscussable, it is time to compromise, and it is time to embrace the words of President John Kennedy: "Ask not what your country can do for you, ask what you can do for your country." If members of Congress, the Super Committee, the Tea Party, and Occupy Wall Street, as well as union leaders, corporate executives, and the American people do not ask what they can do for the betterment of America and its citizens, nothing will happen to reverse these trends, and we all will witness the fall of the United States of America.

We cannot let this happen.

You cannot allow this to happen.

Appendix

Consolidated Restatement and Summary of all Recommendations for Congress

What you are about to read is a list of all the solutions and recommendations that are contained in both the Rebirth of American Greatness and *Death of the American Heart*. I wanted to create a resource section so you, the reader, would have access to a quick listing of recommendations that could be copied and used as a platform for discussion and debate. Listed below are all of the recommendations I would like to submit to Congress and the Super Committee for their consideration. It would be great if we could start a groundswell of ideas that could pour into Congress and have some positive influence on the debates that will be going on during the next four-year presidential cycle. The first list of recommendations is from this new book, *Rebirth of American Greatness*, and the second list is from *Death of the American Heart*.

Recommendations for Congress

1. **Social Security**

   - Congress should immediately raise the retirement age for anyone under fifty to an eligibility age of seventy through 2020.

- For anyone under fifty in 2021, Congress should raise the retirement age to seventy-two.

- For anyone under fifty in 2035, Congress should raise the retirement age to seventy-four.

2. Balanced Budget

- Congress should immediately pass a law requiring the budget to be balanced every year after 2018. This would give our government and politicians five years to get organized and put the necessary discipline and structure in place to support the balanced-budget law.

3. Tax Structure

- A tiered tax system should be instituted, starting in 2015. Individuals who make less than $5,000 per year will not be required to pay federal income tax. Congress should adopt the following tax structure:

  - $1.00–$5,000 = No Tax

  - $5,001–$10,000 = 2%

  - $10,000–$15,000 = 3%

  - $15, 001–$20,000 = 4%

  - $20,001–$40,000 = 10%

- $40,001–$60,000 = 13%

- $60,001–$100,000 = 16%

- $100,001–$250,000 = 17%

- $250,001–$500,000 = 18%

- $500,001–$1,000,000 = 19%

- $1.000,000–$5,000,00 = 20%

- $5,00,001–$10,000,000 = 25%

- $10,000,001+ = 30%

- Tax Deductions—To support the proposed tiered tax structure, all deductions need to be eliminated, including the childcare tax credit, mortgage interest rate tax credit, energy improvements to your home tax credit, education credits, etc. *All* means just that: the elimination of *all* tax credits or incentives. The tax code should not be used to incentivize people to buy things or support political causes or projects such as "cash for clunkers." You should be able to complete your tax filing using a single one-page form from the IRS. It should be that simple. If the government wants to encourage citizens to support various programs and endeavors, they should use a grant system and leave the tax code alone.

- The proposed tax structure is very simple. Again, you make X and you pay Y.

- This new tax structure should free up a lot of staff employees at the Internal Revenue Service. Some of these employees can be downsized, while other IRS employees should be redeployed to focus on Medicare and Medicaid fraud as well as welfare and SSI fraud and waste.

- The corporate tax rate should be reduced to 20%. This rate should also apply to profits generated from overseas operations. However, if a corporation decides to repatriate those profits and invest in new plants, equipment, and research and development in the United States, the tax rate on those repatriated profits should be 5%–10% since those profits will be used to create jobs in the United States. However, just as the personal income tax proposal listed above, this proposed corporate tax rate needs to be supported by a zero exemptions policy. No loopholes or tax deductions of any kind. To stimulate research and development, we should use a grant-funding program such as we currently use to fund certain university research projects.

- Since I am not an economist, the proposed tax structures for both individuals and corporations will need to be massaged, analyzed, and vetted to ensure fairness.

4.   Earmarks

- There should be an immediate ban on all earmarks. Nothing should be added onto a bill. The philosophy in Congress should be "one bill, one vote." No attaching special appropriations to a bill. Every piece of legislation should stand on its own merit. We can create a budget for each committee to utilize for special appropriations or projects. However, each special appropriation or project will need to be discussed in committee and receive a majority vote. Every appropriation or project that is funded by a committee needs to be made public. Once again, no appropriations, earmarks, or special projects should be added to another bill.

5.   Health Care

- The Affordable Care Act—or what a lot of people refer to as Obama Care—should be repealed immediately. A comprehensive health care plan is needed, but the current bill was flawed from the very beginning. The majority of American citizens did not want this particular health care reform program to become legislation; their demands ranged from killing the bill outright to redesigning the bill. Here is what the Super Committee should have recommended:

  - First, we need to repeal the health care reform act.

- Next, we must initiate major reforms to our tort system and put a cap on lawsuits. The current legal system is broken and is forcing many good doctors to leave their practices because of malpractice insurance costs and the number of lawsuits that certain lawyers are filing against them as practitioners.

- Once we have reformed our legal system, we need to aggressively address Medicare and Medicaid fraud. This type of fraud is costing the taxpayers hundreds of billions of dollars each year. It is blatant, out in the open, and we are not doing enough to stop it. I recommend that we unleash the IRS on the doctors, health care providers, hospitals, and clinics that are suspected of cheating the system. We can use technology to map and analyze claims and spot trends. As a result of the new tax structure put in place by Congress, many IRS agents will be available for redeployment to the front lines to fight fraud.

- One more major recommendation to address Medicare and Medicaid fraud is to establish mandatory jail sentences for people convicted of fraud. No plea deals; once a doctor, nurse, technician, office manager, or executive is convicted of fraud, he or she will go right to jail.

- Concurrent with the tort reform and fraud initiatives, we should have a joint committee redesign our health care system. This should entail taking the best parts of the current health care reform act and making the changes necessary to have a comprehensive plan that meets the needs of the average American citizen. No behind-closed-door negotiations, no input from lobbyists. No special exemptions for unions, corporations or other special-interest groups. Everyone will be required to participate in the plan, even Congress. Everything must be transparent and presented to the American people before any votes are taken.

- Finally, a new Super Committee should be created to focus only on health care reform. Too many Americans have been denied medical care by insurance companies because of previous conditions. Too many Americans have lost their insurance because they were laid off, and they find it very hard to get appropriate coverage while they are unemployed. Serious study should be given to a single-payer concept and insurance that people do not lose when they lose their jobs.

6. Downsizing/Rightsizing Federal Government

- A cabinet-level effectiveness review of every major program in each Secretary's area of responsibility should be instituted immediately.

- Redundant operations, agencies, tasks, and positions should be eliminated. The goal is to reduce the size of the federal government by 30 percent, in other words to the level it was when Bill Clinton first took office as president.

- Technology should be incorporated and self-service kiosks implemented to reduce the amount of paperwork and the number of forms generated by government regulations.

- Growth of the federal government should be capped at 25% of the growth of our gross domestic product (GDP). For instance, if our GDP is 4% the government growth could not exceed 1%. If we have zero GDP growth, then the federal government could not expand.

7. Lobbyists

- All lobbyists should be banned from Washington and required to conduct their business with senators and congressional representatives in the state offices.

- Every lobbyist's visit to a senator's or representative's office should be made public, regarding who visited and the purpose of the visit. This information can be printed in the local newspaper or made available on the official's website. Transparency must be a requirement for all interactions with lobbyists.

- Senior-level federal government employees must be banned from lobbying members of Congress for a period of five years after they have left office.

8. Congressional Reform

- The congressional staff should be reduced by 30 percent.

- Senators and congressmen and women must be required to follow all the same laws that American citizens are required to follow. There must be no exemptions.

- Members of Congress should have the same health care and retirement plans as other federal employees.

- Revised term limits should be instituted, starting in 2016 with the presidential election. The president's term in office should be six years, a congressional representative's should be four years, and a senator's should be six years. This way nobody has to worry about getting reelected. Elections can be structured so that a third of the Senate changes every two years and half the House changes every two years.

- We should explore the possibility of doing away with the House of Representatives as we know it today. A panel should be commissioned to investigate the plausibility of reengineering our legislative branch of government to eliminate the House and expand the Senate. Is it possible for the legislative branch of our government to consist only of the Senate? What if we had five or six senators from each state instead of having House members as well as two senators? Could we dramatically reduce the bureaucracy, streamline the process of government, and reduce operating costs? I include this idea only as an interesting concept to think about and as an example of the type of breakthrough thinking the Super Committee should have engaged in regarding the quest to cut $1.5 trillion in ten years. Everything needs to be on the table for discussion. No sacred cows.

9. Deficit Reduction

- Congress needs to pass a law that requires the deficit to be eliminated by 2022. This would give the federal government sufficient time to manage its affairs and get its house in order. Whether by a constitutional amendment or a law, we need to transition to a debt-free nation by 2022. We should allow a deficit only if we are engaged in another war, we experience a major act of terrorism, or we need to deal with a horrific natural disaster with a significant infrastructural loss that needs to be replaced ASAP.

- Congress shall discipline the various agencies to spend only what they have budgeted to spend. Agencies and their employees should be incentivized to save money through process-improvement initiatives and rewarded when they come in under budget. The federal government will spend only what it takes in from its various revenue sources.

10. Foreign Aid

- Congress should immediately pass a law that halts all foreign aid. We should continue to supply food, medicine, and clean water to friendly nations. We should not give aid to any country that does not like us, support us, or help us deal with global challenges such as Russia's and China's refusal to support the UN resolution to halt the killing of innocent civilians in Syria. As a result of these countries' refusal to support us, thousands more innocent men, women, and children were slaughtered.

- We should immediately stop all aid to Pakistan, which is working against us and, by its support of the Taliban, has indirectly contributed to the deaths of many of our servicemen and women in Afghanistan.

- We should also stop all foreign aid to China because it is not playing by the rules when it comes to global trade.

11. Fanny Mae & Freddie Mac

- Congress should prevent the payment of legal fees to the former Fanny Mae and Freddie Mac executives who are charged with crimes.

- Congress should also abolish both Fanny and Freddie as quasi-government institutions. No taxpayer money should go to these organizations, and the government should go after the executives, current and former, to recapture some of the outlandish bonus money they were paid for managing these organizations into a state of deep decline.

12. Energy Policy

- Congress should craft a comprehensive energy policy and send it to the president for his signature. We should open up all sites for drilling that have been identified as being viable oil-producing sites, including offshore sites and those in Alaska, Texas, and the Dakotas.

- Our energy policy should include the use of coal wherever possible, with government grants being given for the development of clean-coal technologies.

- A new generation of nuclear power plants should be built with a fast-track permitting process.

- At the same time, the government needs to fund research for the development of alternative clean energy for our future requirements. However, we must exploit our current fossil-fuel resources as well as our nuclear resources until the clean-energy_alternatives become a viable source.

- China is currently going around the world signing oil deals to make sure it has the necessary energy to continue to grow and prosper as a nation with the strongest economy in the world. We cannot let China out-negotiate us in the oil market. We also need to drill in our own backyard to reach a state of oil independence as a nation and not be held hostage by the Middle East and countries that teach their children to hate Americans.

- We should immediately eliminate all subsidies to the oil companies. The top five oil companies had combined profits last year of approximately $137 billion. We should encourage drilling and exporting so the oil companies can continue to be success, and at the same time we should redirect their tens of billions of dollars in subsidies each year to help pay down our national debt.

13. National Manufacturing Policy

- Congress should create a robust national manufacturing policy, designed to protect our core manufacturing industries and entice companies to bring some of their outsourced operations back to the United States. The current global marketplace does not have a level playing field. Some countries, such as China, do not play by the rules. Other factors—such as our tax policy, environmental rules, enormous amounts of forms and paperwork, and the various regulations our manufactures must comply with—put our companies at a competitive disadvantage.

- Congress needs to pull together a committee, consisting of the best academic and business minds, to help craft a manufacturing policy that will level the global playing field and eliminate the barriers that prevent our manufacturers from being competitive.

- As I noted in my first book, *Death of the American Heart*, Congress needs to establish manufacturing enterprise zones in the poorest and most disadvantaged communities in the United States. Special tax incentives (reduced tax rates) should be given to any company that brings back a plant or operations that had been outsourced. The returning operations should be located within these newly created enterprise zones and would receive a substantial reduction in the tax rate on profits generated from these repatriated operations for some period of time (twenty years, for example). Some of you may recall the exodus of pharmaceutical companies that established operations in Puerto Rico and Ireland to take advantage of a twenty-year tax break. It is very possible for us to experience the same dynamic if we create the right type of incentives for companies to use these enterprise zones.

Our new manufacturing policy should require from our politicians, business leaders, and union officials the following:

Our politicians need to

- Create a tax policy that encourages investment in new plants, equipment, automation, and technology. This tax policy should apply to profits generated both within the United States and in other countries.

- Create incentives for companies to bring outsourced operations back from overseas and relocated them in our most depressed communities.

- Develop a policy that restricts governmental agencies like the EPA from placing new regulations on business without congressional approval.

- Review all current regulations, policies, requirements, forms, and procedures, and eliminate those that are not adding value.

- Create policies that make it easy to do business with the United States.

- Place a 20% tax on all products imported from China.

Our business leaders need to:

- Look at investing in robotics and automation to upgrade their facilities.

- Use outsourcing only as a last strategy. They need to explore lower-cost alternatives within the United States before they look to Asia or South America.

- Refrain from paying bonuses or giving salary increases to executives who have generated profits on operations they have outsourced.

- Force their purchasing departments to buy American-made products, sub-assemblies, and raw materials whenever available if the price is not too far out of line.

- Implement formal cost-reductions programs in every one of their factories, offices, or operations.

- Be willing to trade off some small measure of profit for the social good of the community before deciding to close a plant or operation.

- Set a long-term strategic goal, if they are big warehouse-type retailers, to require 50 percent of the products they sell to be made in America.

- Ensure that big electronic-device and computer-manufacturing companies manufacture no more than 50 percent of their products outside the United States. This 50 percent balance should also apply to IT, software engineering, web design, call centers, R&D, and other administrative functions.

Our union officials need to

- Be flexible and willing to change work rules and procedures so the company can become more competitive and productive.

- Be willing to give wage and benefit concessions rather than being rigid and forcing the company to go to China.

- Participate with management as partners in the process of trying to keep plants open. This will require management to invite the union officials into their strategic discussions and planning activities as trusted partners.

- Encourage innovation by their members that will reduce operating costs and improve productivity.

- Encourage their members to work hard and be flexible.

- Embrace operational advances such as robotics and automation.

14. White House Czars

- Congress should recommend the elimination of all White House Czars and their respective staffs.

- Congress should pass a law that requires anyone nominated by the president for a position in government to have a swift up or down vote. No playing politics and manipulating the nomination process to satisfy petty personal agendas. Let each nominee receive a swift yea or nay vote.

15. Welfare Reform

- Congress should recommend comprehensive welfare reform. This reform should include a complete overhaul of the various areas that are subject to the largest amount of fraud and waste, such as food stamps, SSI, "Section 8" housing, and so on. We are a compassionate people, when compassion is justified.

16. Right to Work

- Congress should pass a law giving all American citizens the right to work anywhere and on any given government contract, private enterprise, or public organization. American workers, companies, and organizations of all types have been bullied by union leaders who are responsible for at least part of the drive to outsource American jobs to low-cost labor markets such as China, India, and Mexico. Unions' rigid work rules, their resistance to accept needed changes, and their refusal to respond to the dynamics of the new global market have put America at a competitive disadvantage. When Boeing wanted to relocate part of its manufacturing operation from Washington State to South Carolina, a right-to-work state, the company was told that it could not, and the government would take them to court to stop them from doing so. Who was driving this insanity? The unions, of course, because they wanted to keep union jobs in Washington. Apparently it is perfectly okay to let Boeing send its manufacturing operations overseas but it is not okay to allow them to send their operations to South Carolina. Given the current economic situation in this country, this move on the part of the unions and government bureaucrats defies logic.

17. Term Limits

- We need term limits that eliminate the need for reelection campaigns. When we elect people to Congress for a two-year term they basically never get out of their reelection mentality and they become susceptible to being held hostage by the special-interest groups and lobbyists who contributed to their campaigns.

- The president of the United States should be elected for one term of six years. If the president cannot achieve his or her agenda in six years, two more years will not matter.

- Senators should be elected for one term of six years. The election process could be phased in so that every two years, one-third of the Senate will change.

- Congressional representatives should be elected for one term of four years. This supports the intent of our Founding Fathers to send average citizens to Congress and then have them return to their communities. No more career politicians.

18. Reengineering our Federal Government

- We should also reengineer the role of our federal government to bring it back into alignment with the vision of our Founding Fathers and the constitutional intent. This effort should include a complete review of all federal agencies and the various programs they support, to determine if they are absolutely necessary. If they are deemed not to be a mission-critical agency or program then they should immediately be eliminated.

The recommendations I have included above represent my thoughts on what Congress and the Super Committee should have discussed during their strategic brainstorming and planning sessions. What I have included below are my key thoughts and recommendations that were contained in my first book, *Death of the American Heart*. I have included them in this book to capture, in one place, all the recommendations that I have personally brainstormed and identified as potential solutions to some of the political, social, and financial challenges facing our nation today. They may not all make sense to you, and certainly I do not expect you to agree with all of them. I have not vetted these ideas or empirically researched their applicability. However, they do represent the type of out-of-box thinking that needs to take place to change the paradigm in

Washington, DC, and allow our political and business leaders to create the bold reforms and changes necessary to transform our nation back to a state of greatness. The recommendations from my first book are as follows:

19. The president of the United States and Congress shall create a new national vision for America that will act as the engine for change and transformation, allowing our nation to once again achieve a state of greatness like the one that President Kennedy created in the '60s. Through President Kennedy's vision of putting a man on the moon, he put America in first place as the greatest nation that ever existed. The ball rests in the president's court to craft such a vision and have Congress approve it as the driving force and beacon of light as our nation aspires to achieve its goals.

20. The president of the United States and Congress should create a core set of shared national values that will permeate every corner of our society and touch every citizen. These shared values should be reflected in the behavior of all American citizens, regardless of age, profession, economic status, religion, or political affiliation. These values should be reflected in all policies and laws that are developed by our federal, state, and local governments.

21. Businesses and organizations of all types will need to embrace these shared values in their interactions with clients, customers, consumers, employees, business partners, suppliers, key stakeholders, and constituents.

22. Schools, colleges, and universities must create institutions that support, reflect, and reinforce these shared values as they go about the business of educating our children, young men and women, and future leaders of our nation. Values, ethics, and personal integrity should be included in the core-teaching curriculum for all grade levels.

23. We must maintain our traditions and holidays as a nation, and be tolerant and supportive of the cultural diversity and unique traditions of the various groups that represent the tapestry of our citizenry.

24. We should be able to make room for the various gods our citizens worship as we pursue our national vision. There should always be room for one's god on our journey to sustained greatness as a world leader.

25. The president of the United States and Congress must develop a set of strategies that will rebuild our manufacturing base. These strategies should include the creation of a tax policy that will help attract manufacturing back to the United States and is business-friendly.

26. Enterprise manufacturing "no tax" zones should be established in the hundred most impoverished communities in the United States. Extra tax incentives should be given to any company that returns to the United States the manufacture of products and the operation of services that were previously outsourced to offshore vendors.

27. The president of the United States and Congress should create a law requiring that the budget be balanced. No deficit spending should be allowed. This law should also mandate a "one item, one bill" requirement. No more pork or add-on projects should be allowed. Each appropriation should stand on its own merits.

28. There should be mandatory prison sentences for politicians, lobbyists, and business leaders doing business with the government who are convicted of corruption. These convicted individuals should serve hard time—no more country-club prisons.

29. Congress should rewrite the tax code to be a flat tax for both individuals and businesses—no more special deductions. You make X, you pay Y—no more writing off your vacation home, boat, trips, etc.

30. Utilizing the available technology, we should downsize the federal government by at least 30 percent. We should reengineer every federal agency and eliminate those that do not add value anymore, are redundant, or do not meet the means test for being critical to the core mission and purpose of the federal government. We should shift as many services as possible to Internet transactions.

31. We should immediately reengineer our kindergarten-through-twelfth-grade educational systems. We should start by significantly reducing the bureaucracy of the US Department of Education and recharter the agency with creating the necessary protocols, policies, and actions that will position our children as the most educated in the world, with top rankings in math, science, and technology. This redesign should include the creation of a two-track system, one track being academically oriented and the other technology oriented. The technology track should include studies in green technology, biotechnology, computer technology, chemistry, physics, and science.

32. As soon as our children are toilet trained, we should start their basic educational process, which will include a foundation in reading, math, science, technology, and a foreign language.

33. The US Department of Education should be downsized and the freed-up assets reallocated to the states for the purpose of creating centers of educational excellence, especially in high-crime, high-poverty, and high-dropout areas.

34. To be eligible for the reallocated funds, each state must reduce the ratio of administrative personnel to teachers. Each senior-level administrative person must teach one class per semester.

35. In addition to stimulating the minds of our children, we should also work on building physically fit and healthy students at all grade levels. Physical activity and good nutrition should be built into the curriculum at all grade levels.

36. The school day should be lengthened to match that of other nations with which we are competing in the global

marketplace. This will also allow our schools to develop intramural sports programs in which all students must participate during the school week.

37. Teachers must participate in mandatory training each year that meets specific knowledge standards, and they should receive performance evaluations based on results. If they don't meet the knowledge standards and their classroom performance is below par, they should be put on a developmental plan to correct their performance. After one semester, if they have not improved their performance, they should be placed on developmental probation designed to increase their level of competence. If after two full school years their performance has not improved substantially, they should be terminated.

38. We should immediately issue a mandate for the United Nations to reform and eliminate corruption. The UN should be required to restructure itself to become more effective and efficient. Just like our federal government, the United Nations must conduct an agency-by-agency performance review and eliminate any agency or part thereof that is not adding value to the citizens of the world. The United States should start to reduce its contribution to the UN by 20 percent per year if there are no substantial signs of reform.

39. Congress should pass laws that are aimed at reforming our legal system. Strong tort reform should be mandated, with the goals of eliminating frivolous lawsuits, streamlining our judicial process, capping damages awarded, and placing accountability for one's personal actions in the process. Medical malpractice laws should be established to bring fairness and sensibility into the process, which will not adversely affect good doctors.

40. Stiff, swift, and mandatory penalties should be established to curb the Medicare and Medicaid fraud that is currently rampant in the system. Violators should be sent to jail quickly. The government needs to redirect some assets from other agencies to identify the most corrupted areas of the country, and with a SWAT-like mentality make the necessary interventions to put the cheats in jail.

41. We need to restructure how we provide foreign aid to other countries. We should place a moratorium on all financial foreign aid for a two-year period. No money should be given to any country during this time. Instead of providing money during these two years, we will continue to provide food, medicine, and technical support as needed, but financial payments should stop. During this period, we should profile the needs of our own country regarding roads, bridges, light rail, hospitals, and school upgrades, and allocate some of these earmarked foreign-aid funds to improve our own infrastructure. We will not give money to dictators and government leaders who oppress, torture, or disrespect their citizens. Instead, we will use other channels to provide food, medicine, and infrastructure support.

42. We must allow our traditions and holidays to be honored in all our facilities. We need to reverse the trend

of being too politically correct and allow our children, for instance, to celebrate Christmas, Hanukkah, etc., in schools and other public places throughout our great land.

43. Congress must create a law that prohibits add-ons and pork to bills. We need a "one item, one bill" law. Congress can create other mechanisms for dealing with special projects using the conference committee and subcommittee infrastructure. Major legislation must stand on its own and not be hijacked with pork spending projects as legally attached parasites.

44. Congress and the president of the United States must maintain a balanced budget. No more deficit spending.

45. The silent majority needs to become more active and form the basis for a viable third party.

46. We are no longer at war with Germany or Japan, so why not close our foreign military bases? We could save tens of billions of dollars a year if we closed 50 percent of our bases overseas. All of this money could be allocated for education and enterprise manufacturing zones. The Cold War is over, and a new strategic defensive plan regarding global bases needs to be developed.

47. We must stop trying to purge God and patriotism from the lives of our children. The framers of our Constitution identified the issues with the separation of church and state, but we have gone way too far in trying to be politically correct.

Bring back school prayer and have our children not only say the Pledge of Allegiance to the flag, but sing "The Star-Spangled Banner" every day. We should make it okay to talk about the heroes of our past, and to honor and respect the men and women who wear our country's uniform.

48. A Potential National Vision

The United States of America will strive to become the most compassionate, caring and supportive nation in the world. Our citizens will be the most educated workforce on the planet and will dedicate themselves to improving the quality of life for all humankind. We will lead the world in the development of technology. Whether it is medicine, food, clean water, energy, science, or transportation, we will develop and deploy these technologies throughout the world.

49. A Recommended Set of National Global Operating Principles

In our dealing with other nations, we will:

- Teach and not tell

- Counsel and not criticize

- Value and not vanquish

- Support and not scold

- Respect diversity and not try to force compliance

- Lead and not manage

- Promote a hand and not a handout

- Be forthright and honest and not deceiving

- Earn respect and not command respect

- Help and not forget

- Cure and not confuse

- Feed and not ignore

- Tolerate and not condemn

- Cherish and not control

- Love and not hate

50.   A Possible set of National Core Shared Values

It is very important for me to clarify what I mean by a set of national core values. I can hear the critics now, saying, "How dare he recommend a set of values? Who does he think he is? Whose values are they, and what if I don't agree with these values?" I ask you to hold off on your judgment and criticism of my belief that we need to embrace and constantly reinforce a set of national core values that are taught from the day our children are born to the day they die. So please open your mind to at least exploring these values in the context of where our nation is currently—how Americans are living their lives and conducting themselves at work and in society. For every value that I list there are thousands of Americans who are living those values every day and just as fellow citizens who are not demonstrating those values. I will first list the core values that I believe will strengthen the cultural fabric of our great nation if they are taught and constantly reinforced at home and throughout our school system. Second, I will add some additional context which I will import from *Death of the American Heart*. The following are the core values I believe should be part of the American cultural fabric:

- Respect

- Loyalty

- Honesty

- Integrity

- Hard work

- Dedication

- Commitment

- Sharing

- Helping others

- Compassion and caring

- Personal responsibility

It is my strong belief that if there were more emphasis in our country on values, religion, and the various gods that represents the major religions, there would be a profound and positive impact on the behavior of future generations of adults in the United States. I also believe that teenage pregnancy would decline significantly and high school dropout rates, especially those of our minority students, would fall rapidly. Personal integrity and honesty would reassert itself in our academic, government, and business communities and relationships. I deeply believe that there would be a greater appreciation of diversity, a more willing attitude to help others in need, and an increased kindness to others, regardless of their lots in life or their background. In the long term, I think we would see a significant reduction of corruption among our government officials and business leaders.

For people who do not believe in God or have no affiliation with a religion, this is not a problem, because the values that our Founding Fathers espoused and the values I have listed above are universal in their association to all of humankind, and they apply to everyone in our country.

- Wouldn't you like to see the prison population in the United States decrease, especially the number of black and Hispanic young men?

- Wouldn't you like to see our elected representatives demonstrate a higher order of personal integrity?

- Wouldn't you like to see our business leaders and union leaders operate with a greater amount of openness and honesty in their transactions?

- Wouldn't it be great if our entertainers and sports heroes were outstanding role models for our youth to emulate?

- Wouldn't it be great to know that our young men and women embodied truth and decency in their interactions?

All of these things are possible if we embrace a value-driven philosophy throughout our society. A society that does not embrace a set of core operating principles will produce a society of misfits and socially irresponsible, self-centered, greedy, uncaring citizens. How could you argue that the values listed above are not an appropriate way to behave and conduct your life?

These values are the basic core elements of how we should treat each other, regardless of whether we believe in a God, Mother Nature, some other force in the universe, or just ourselves. If you disagree with these universal values, then what will you espouse as your central theme in life regarding how you behave, treat others, and function in our society? What would your values look like?

- If you could not embrace respect, would you be disrespectful to others?

- If you could not demonstrate loyalty, would you be disloyal to your family, friends, and employer?

- If you could not embrace honesty, would you lie and cheat your way through life?

- If you could not model integrity, would you allow yourself to engage in inappropriate behavior?

- If you could not work hard but are capable, would you be a slacker and have others pull your share?

- If you could not be dedicated, would you go through life without a purpose and sense of meaning?

- If you could not exercise commitment, would your word and handshake mean nothing in life's transactions?

- If you could not share, would you hoard and only take but never give of yourself?

- If you would not help others, would you become consumed with satisfying yourself and your personal needs and give nothing back to society?

- If you could not embrace compassion and caring for others, would you be so narcissistic that you thought only of your own comfort, wealth, power, and status?

- If you could not assume personal responsibility for your actions, words, and deeds, would you go through life blaming everyone else for your shortcomings, failures, and mistakes?

These are not the values of any one particular religion; instead they represent universal values that frame how people should treat others and conduct their lives on this earth. These are the values that need to be reinforced in our schools, religious institutions, businesses, and government organizations, and generally throughout the core of our society.

I hope that the above descriptions put in context how important values are in shaping our nation's culture. They must be articulated and reinforced throughout our educational system, business community, and public institutions to have a positive shaping effect on our culture and society.

Finally I would like the president and members of Congress to consider what I call a national set of aspirations that are derived from our vision, operating principles, and core values. These are higher-level goals or results of our new national focus.

51.   Potential List of National Aspirations

In our future society our vision, operating principles, and core values will allow us to

- Educate everyone

- Feed the hungry

- Help the poor

- Cure the sick

- Eliminate crime as we know it

- Establish values throughout the land

- Be guided by morality

- Be honest in all our dealings

- Fix the systems that serve our citizens

- Provide good jobs for everyone

- Raise our standard of living

- Become exceptional stewards of the environment

As you can gather from reading this book, there is a lot of over-lap and redundancy when it comes to potential solutions to our na-tion's most serious problems. This is important in my eyes_because it solidifies many recommendations as having substantial merit, at least enough merit to engender a conversation. However, because of the current polarization of our two political parties and the pressures from special-interest groups, these recommendations will never reach the floor of Congress for debate unless you, the reader, create your own list of things you think need to change and send that to the Super Committee, the president, and your congressional representatives. In addition, I have one other simple request: please identify the recom-mendations or solutions that you believe would make a difference in helping our nation solve some of its major challenges, and use the power of your social network to communicate these solutions to your network contacts and your congressional representatives. We can use the power of the web and social networking to apply pressure on

Congress to get serious about reforms before it is too late and we yield our global economic and technical leadership to China and India.

If you get involved and get your social network involved, it will be possible to once again develop a society of people who care for one another and are willing to help advance the standard of living and the quality of life for all Americans. We can, and I believe we will, continue to create the greatest society on the planet—if we embrace the necessary reforms to bring the pendulum back into the center of American life.

About the Author

Peter Hughes is President and Chief Executive Officer of High Performance Leadership, Ltd. He is the founder of the OD Think Tank, HPL University, Global Leadership Institute, and Service Delivery Leadership Institute, and cofounder of the High Performance Leadership Center. These organizations provide management education, organizational development, and business consulting services focusing on creating outstanding leadership and group behaviors within organizations. Peter also specializes in developing highly effective teams, change management consulting, and process improvement.

Peter has consulted with a broad base of companies, industries, and institutions in the areas of academia, pharmaceuticals, medical devices, computers, software, the Internet, web design, retail, banking, traditional manufacturing, independent distribution, and government, in the United States, Europe, South America, and Asia. He has designed and implemented organizational development interventions for these organizations that focused on areas such as leadership development, team building, process reengineering, new product development, customer satisfaction, total quality, management education, executive coaching, and building a more positive culture.

Peter's education includes a master's degree in education specializing in management and organizational development from Antioch University, Cambridge, Massachusetts, with undergraduate studies at Temple University in the area of industrial management. He is a past winner of the Johnson & Johnson Company's Claude V. Swank Manufacturing Excellence Award for outstanding performance in the areas of quality, cost, and productivity. He is also the recipient of three Presidential Commendations from President Reagan's Committee on the Employment of Disabled Youth due to his efforts in teaching job interviewing and assimilation skills to disabled students and in curriculum development. He was featured in the Handling and Shipping Management Magazine for the results of his work in reengineering Millipore Corporations World Wide Distribution Center.

Peter has been affiliated with Cambridge College for the past ten years as a senior faculty member teaching graduate-level courses and seminars in leadership, operations management, and organizational development. He also is a part-time faculty member at the University of New Hampshire's Whittemore School of Business and Economics, where he teaches organizational behavior.

Peter published his first book, *Death of the American Heart*, in February 2011. He is currently working on his third book, which will be on leadership and high-performing teams.

www.ingramcontent.com/pod-product-compliance
Lightning Source LLC
Chambersburg PA
CBHW070015300526
45794CB00001B/325